MW01164837

Low-cost Private Education

Low-cost Private Education

Impacts on Achieving Universal Primary Education

Edited by

Bob Phillipson

Commonwealth Secretariat

Commonwealth Secretariat
Marlborough House
Pall Mall
London SW1Y 5HX
United Kingdom

© Commonwealth Secretariat 2008

All rights reserved. No part of this publication may be reproduced, stored in a retrieval system, or transmitted in any form or by any means, electronic or mechanical, including photocopying, recording or otherwise without the permission of the publisher.

Published by the Commonwealth Secretariat
Edited by Jane Lanigan
Designed by SJI Services
Cover design by Tattersall Hammarling & Silk
Index by Indexing Specialists (UK) Ltd
Printed by Hobbs the Printers Ltd, Totton, Hampshire

Views and opinions expressed in this publication are the responsibility of the authors and should in no way be attributed to the institutions to which they are affiliated or to the Commonwealth Secretariat.

Wherever possible, the Commonwealth Secretariat uses paper sourced from sustainable forests or from sources that minimise a destructive impact on the environment.

Cover photo: Stuart Freedman/Panos Pictures

Copies of this publication may be obtained from

The Publications Section
Commonwealth Secretariat
Marlborough House
Pall Mall
London SW1Y 5HX
United Kingdom
Tel: +44 (0)20 7747 6534
Fax: +44 (0)20 7839 9081
Email: publications@commonwealth.int
Web: www.thecommonwealth.org/publications

A catalogue record for this publication is available from the British Library.

ISBN (paperback): 978-0-85092-880-8
ISBN (e-book): 978-1-84859-004-5

Contents

Editor's Dedication

This book is dedicated to the work and memory of
Ian Smith (1955–2008)

Foreword

The non-state sector is playing an increasing role in the delivery of education in a number of developing countries that are still striving to attain Education for All (EFA) and the education Millennium Development Goals (MDGs). 'Non-state' is a term that presents its own problems of clear definition and focus. Broadly, it can be used to describe formal institutions independent of government administration, including philanthropically subsidised and faith-based schools, education delivered by not-for-profit non-governmental organisations (NGOs), community schools, and fee-paying private institutions. In many instances the latter classification is used interchangeably with the term non-state, especially as the recent growth in developing countries is happening amongst private providers. But the distinction between the different sectors is important as the dynamics of each have an impact on factors relating to access and quality issues, among others.

Private institutions for elite groups in society have been in evidence at all levels of the education system, while NGO, philanthropic and faith-based providers have been catering for poorer communities in many Commonwealth countries pre-independence. More recently, NGOs have been playing an increasing role in the implementation of donor education projects. However, it is fee paying non-state primary and secondary schools – previously associated with wealth and privilege – that have recently been playing an increasing role since the 1990s in parts of Commonwealth South Asia, Sub-Saharan Africa and the Caribbean. This is a new low-cost incarnation targeted at much broader numbers.

With the EFA and MDG commitment of many countries towards 2015, the pressure on education systems to provide quality education for all has heightened the debate.

Evidence indicates that low cost private schools at the primary and secondary level have mushroomed in some of the poorest areas of Africa and Asia. These are often concentrated in the shanty towns (or 'informal settlements') of urban centres. While private sector schools may continue to carry the stigma of profit-making enterprise, their existence must be seriously considered given the limitations of many government educational systems in providing universal access.

The private sector is not only potentially more responsive to excess demand; another perceived benefit could be the setting of price according to the ability to pay, arguably engendering both cost-effectiveness and accountability. With many poor families unable to meet state school fees and/or other 'hidden' costs, such as school uniforms, books, etc., a competitive private alternative presents opportunities that some countries cannot meet at present.

This study has attempted to consider the impact of these private schools on access to education for the poor, the status of national enrolment rates, the quality of education, and transition to secondary school.

The growth of private schools has not been limited to countries where school fees and other costs still exist. In response to the challenge of meeting EFA and the MDGs, several countries within the Commonwealth abolished school fees, leading to an expansion of demand beyond the capacity of the system. With teacher shortages resulting in high pupil–teacher ratios and insufficient resources and physical infrastructure, the poorest communities have been the ones to suffer the most, leading to either lack of faith in what is available from public providers.

The report concludes by emphasising that private schools do play an important role in achieving education for all alongside state funded programmes. Public education alone may not be adequate to guarantee all children access to quality education because of resource constraints in the public sector. It is these gaps in public education that private schools fill. Private schools can help to achieve EFA through proper regulation, supervision and government support in both financial and material terms.

The Commonwealth Secretariat is grateful to Buani Consulting for conducting the research that resulted in this report, and especially to the late Ian Smith who provided the introduction and the international context sections. Sadly Ian died while this volume was being prepared. We are also grateful to the other contributors, and particularly to Bob Phillipson who coordinated the report on which the book is based, and who acted as editor of the book itself.

Finally I wish to recognise the contribution of colleagues at the Secretariat who contributed to this activity, Fatimah Kelleher and Florence Malinga.

Dr Henry Kaluba
Head and Advisor, Education
Social Transformation Programmes Division

List of acronyms

ADEPTS	Advancement of Educational Performance Through Teacher Support (India)
AIE	Alternative and innovative education
ASER	Annual Status of Education Report (India)
BRAC	Bangladesh Rural Advancement Committee
BOD	Board of Directors
CRS	Catholic Relief Services
CCT	Centre Co-ordination Tutor (Uganda)
CPD	Continuous professional development
DHS	Demographic and Health Survey
DFID	Department for International Development (UK)
DEO	District Education Officer
DISE	District Information System for Education (India)
ECD	Early Childhood Development
EDI	Educational Development Index
EQUIP	Educational Quality Improvement Programme
EFA	Education for All
EMIS	Education Management Information System
FCT	Federal Capital Territory (Nigeria)
GPI	Gender Parity Index
GoI	Government of India
GER	Gross enrolment rate
IDP	Internally-displaced people
JSS	Junior secondary school
LCU	Local Currency Units
LGEA	Local Government Education Authority (Nigeria)
MTBF	Medium-Term Budget Framework (Uganda)
MDG	Millennium Development Goal
MoES	Ministry of Education and Sports (Uganda)

MLA	Monitoring of Learning Achievement (Nigeria)
NCERT	National Council of Educational Research and Training (India)
NSS	National Sample Surveys
NER	Net enrolment ratio
NEMIS	Nigerian Education Management Information System
NUT	Nigeria Union of Teachers
NGO	Non-governmental organisation
OECD	Organisation for Economic Co-operation and Development
PTA	Parent Teacher Association
PIASCY	Presidential Initiative on AIDS Strategy for Communication to Youth (Uganda)
PLE	Primary leaving examination
PTC	Primary Teachers College
PQTR	Pupil-qualified-teacher ratio
PTR	Pupil-teacher ratio
SSA	*Sarva Shiksha Abhiyan* (India)
SC	Scheduled caste (India)
ST	Scheduled tribe (India)
SFG	School Facilities Grant (Uganda)
SEC	Socio-economic class
SEMIS	State Education Management Information System (Nigeria)
UDES	Uganda DHS EdData Survey
UDHS	Uganda Demographic Household Survey
USh	Uganda Shillings
UNICEF	United Nations Children's Fund
UPE	Universal Primary Education
UP	Uttar Pradesh

1

General Introduction

In recent years, countries around the developing world have introduced universal primary education programmes in an attempt to meet the Millennium Development Goal on education by 2015. This has involved intense expansion of government education systems. One consequence of these programmes has been a dramatic growth in the size of the private education sector and in particular, the emergence of a private education institution that charges a fee that is low enough to be affordable by poor families. These institutions are increasingly being seen as a popular alternative to the public education system. This book aims to investigate this low-cost private education sector and its impact on the goal of achieving universal primary education in India, Nigeria and Uganda.

Defining precisely what we mean by a 'low-cost private school' is easier to do in terms of what it is not rather than what it is. It is not a school run by a non-governmental organisation for charitable or development purposes. It is not a school run by a religious organisation for the furtherance of a particular set of moral values or beliefs. It is not a school offering an educational advantage to its pupils and charging a high price for the privilege of gaining access to it. Finally, it is not a school set up by the local community until the government agrees to take over ownership. In contrast to these distinctions, the low-cost private school is a school that has been set up and is owned by an individual or individuals for the purpose of making profit.

Government systems for collecting educational information naturally function according to the category into which any given school might fit. Thus arises the first problem we encounter when looking at this particular phenomenon; governments have very little information indeed about how many low-cost private schools there are and the children who attend them. Added to this is the fact that owners of such schools often attempt to remain below the radar of the education authorities, as they fear, rightly or wrongly, that they will attract extra costs and constraints.

The emergence of the low-cost private education sector can be explained by the combination of two factors. The first is a widespread perception that the free education provided by the government is somehow low quality. The second is the entrepreneurial action of individuals who have been quick to identify an opportunity and are willing to operate their school at the subsistence level of business. Added to this is the presence of a surplus of educated labour in the countries being studied (especially in India), in particular trained teachers who cannot find work in the public education system. Their desperation for work allows these low-cost schools to pay them a pitiful wage and thereby make their enterprises viable. This book suggests that the dedication of these teachers is the primary advantage that these low-cost private schools have over their competitors. Assessing the quality of the education provided proved to be a very difficult task. It is clear that both parents and pupils feel like they are getting a better deal than their counterparts in government schools. This constitutes one of the main attractions of this new education provision, although there is very little concrete evidence to suggest the quality is any better or worse.

The methodology of the study highlighted in this book was designed to shed some light on the lack of data on these schools and to estimate the extent to which this sub-sector is currently being under-estimated. This was to be done using three independent methods. First, the researchers in each country were to gain access to the national Education Management Information System (EMIS) data and interrogate it to assess what details were available on low-cost private schools. Secondly, they would compare this data with information gathered from local officials, representatives of teachers unions and school proprietors in the area. Thirdly, the country consultants were to undertake a rapid tour of the area to verify for themselves the number of low-cost private schools to be found there. A series of case studies was also carried out in each location to gain an insight into people's experience of the low-cost private education sector.

India

Private schools have a history of more than two decades in India. A proportion of this sector is recognised by the government, but there has been a particular growth in unrecognised, low-fee private schools in recent years. Both recognised and unrecognised schools are accessed by the poor.

The growth of this sector is so great that its impact can be seen in the slowing down of the growth of the government system. Enrolment in government schools is actually declining in over a quarter of districts in India.

Education in low-fee private schools in India is essentially 'subsistence level' education and a preoccupation with economic survival permeates all activities in such schools. Although difficult to quantify, it is widely reported that children who attend private schools are also enrolled in their local government school. This entitles them to a midday meal and allows them to sit the government-administered end-of-year exams in the government school. This dual enrolment results in considerable wastage in the government system. Resources such as teachers, supplies for meals and a host of other entitlements are provided based on enrolment numbers.

Another impact of this growth of the private school system is that more powerful families are tending to reduce their dependence on the public system. This in turn reduces the accountability that the government school demonstrates, since teachers and officials perceive parents from the most disadvantaged groups as being powerless. This has a disheartening effect on the government system, as it is perceived as being less valued and becomes seen as the poor alternative.

The low-cost private schools featured in this book were found to be more concerned with the staging of education than with its quality. Calling themselves 'English Medium' schools, even when no member of staff can speak nor understand English, and presenting props of education such as books and a computer to visitors in an attempt to prove that they are better than the local government alternative.

What is more, many government schools have subtly begun to ape the practices of private schools in an attempt to stem the flow of pupils. The most worrying example of this is the introduction of English from grade 1, despite a widespread shortage of English language among primary schoolteachers.

In sum, the successful 'selling of the superficial' by the private sector in India has led to a dilution in both the notion and practice of education itself.

Nigeria

The general neglect and collapse of Nigerian public schools in the late 1980s and 1990s led to a dramatic increase in the number of private schools, particularly of the unregistered and unrecognised variety.

The study featured in this book, which took place in 2007, found that enrolments in private schools made up 26.9 per cent of the almost 14,000 enrolments in the public and private schools in the selected areas of study. Thus the private schools' share of enrolment is relatively high at over a quarter of total enrolment in this sample.

Although there are concerns about the quality of tuition provided in some of the private schools, the informants to the study had a positive attitude towards the private sector as a contributor to the goals of Education for All (EFA).

There was a consensus among the informants to the study that there are more unregistered and unrecognised schools than government-recognised, registered schools. Estimates range between 30 per cent and 50 per cent more unregistered/unrecognised schools than registered, recognised schools.

Despite the rhetoric of intent of all three tiers of government in the three sampled states in Nigeria, primary education is not free in public schools. In all the three states, parents buy uniforms, textbooks, exercise books and writing materials for their children and these cost an estimated 4,500 naira (N)[1] per annum and constitute one of the hidden costs of public primary schooling.

All the proprietors of private schools were optimistic that the private education sector would continue to grow, largely because of widespread dissatisfaction with the quality of public schools and the inability of government to build enough schools to address sufficiently the demand for education among the poor.

It is quite clear that private schools do provide access to education for children in poor urban and rural areas of Nigeria. What is more, if their potential is properly harnessed, they can help facilitate the attainment of universal *good-quality* primary education. The policy implication of this is that these schools, whether registered or unregistered, cannot be ignored. The current policy of closing down the latter can be counter-productive in so far as the emergence of these schools is the direct consequence of the failure of public schools to provide access to good-quality primary education to an increasing number of poor people.

Government has so far focused not on supporting low-cost private schools (e.g. through matching grants, provision of instructional materials), but on intimidating their owners and threatening them with closure on the pretext that they do not meet the prescribed minimum standards for the establishment of schools and are therefore of poor quality. This approach is unhelpful and even hypocritical, since many government-owned schools are also of very poor quality but are not threatened with closure.

Uganda

When the Universal Primary Education (UPE) programme in Uganda was started in 1997, the government funded a large number of private schools in peri-urban and rural areas for about four years. This included providing UPE funds for teachers' remuneration, on the condition that the schools' fees do not exceed an agreed level. As classroom construction continued in government/government-aided schools, most private schools lost this funding and the majority of low-cost private schools now charge fees that are higher than the agreed level.

As in other countries, there are hidden costs to both supposedly 'free' government education and to low-cost private education in Uganda. The mean average expenditure on schooling among pupils attending public schools was about one-fifth the mean average for pupils attending non-public schools. The low-cost private schools are, however, mainly in peri-urban areas. Here payment for goods and services is frequently offered in kind, and it occasionally happens that children drop out of 'free' government education and instead attend the local low-cost private school, where their parents can pay the fees partly in materials such as maize or beans. Only 22 per cent of children enrolled in the first year of primary school in 1997 reached the seventh year in 2003. This is mainly attributed to the lack of a midday meal provision and parents' inability to pay for the hidden costs of schooling.

Government schools are overall slightly better resourced in terms of infrastructure, especially in sanitation facilities, compared to private schools. In view of the fact that more people are choosing to send their children to private schools, it seems that they are making up for this lack of infrastructure with dedicated and hardworking staff and an average teacher-pupil ratio of 1:35.

One of the primary factors for choosing to send a child to a low-cost private school in Uganda is the perception that it will give them a better education. Part of this perception is attributable the widespread dissatisfaction that is felt towards government education. There is also, however, a perception that low-cost private schools provide quality education. Anecdotal evidence suggests that lower teacher absenteeism and the lower teacher-pupil ratio in private schools allow teachers to teach more effectively and even offer remedial classes to the slower learners.

The Ugandan government alone may not be able to cope with the demand for basic education, and therefore needs non-state actors such as private individuals, institutions and non-governmental organisations (NGOs) to contribute to achieving the EFA goals. Public education alone may not be adequate to guarantee all children access to quality education because of resource constraints in the public sector. It is these gaps in public education that the private schools fill. Private schools can help to achieve EFA through proper regulation, supervision and government support in both financial and material terms.

Note

1. £1 was equivalent to N232.40 in January 2008.

2

Study Introduction

Purpose

The objective of this book is to investigate the impact of low-cost private sector education on achieving universal primary education in three Commonwealth countries: India, Nigeria and Uganda. The three countries have been chosen because they are reported to have seen high growth of low-cost private education in recent years, running in parallel with publicly-funded efforts to achieve universal primary education.

The book is intended to consider the impact of these private schools on access to education for the poor, the status of national enrolment rates, the quality of education, transition to secondary school and other relevant issues.

The growth of low-cost private schools in slums and villages in some of the world's poorest countries and the willingness of even some of the poorest parents to invest in these services rather than those provided by the government, suggests that the entrepreneurs running these schools have identified significant 'gaps' in the market. This begs the question as to whether this represents a failure on the part of the government to deliver basic services or skilful tailoring of the service by entrepreneurs to meet previously unmet needs.

Defining the low-cost private sector

The terms of reference proposed by the Commonwealth Secretariat suggested the following definition of the study subject:

- 'All fee-paying schools/educational establishments offering basic/primary education independent of the government educational system.'

The terms of reference also suggested that the study might consider private-public partnerships if they were significant. In each of the country studies, the general nature of non-government basic education is analysed in order to understand better the entire phenomenon. It was decided to focus specific case study work on schools that fell into the following definition:

- 'Low-cost private schools owned by an individual(s) or other form of commercial enterprise.'[1]

The reason for this focus is that there are many other types of non-government school. Most of them are not directly offering the poor an alternative service for profit. Their motivation and market niche is different.

Some of the major categories of non-government education provision that the authors consider to be marginal to the study are:

- High-fee private schools serving the affluent (*not for the poor*)

- Schools founded by communities hoping for future government grant aiding (*objective is absorption, not profit*)

- Schools run by religious groups and charitable bodies (*not for profit*)

- Schools run by organisations contracted to deliver services on behalf of government (*indirect*)

High-fee elite private schools are a familiar phenomenon in which the customers are rich and middle-class parents, and the school's superior quality is easily explained by its additional resources and selective intake (both unconscious through the fee barrier and conscious through competitive selection in many such schools).

Communities are often forced to start their own schools because the nearest government school is too far for their children to reach safely. Another motivation can be a desire to have one's own school, one distinct in character from the main government school, which is seen as catering for a particular group (ethnic, religious or caste). However, in each of these cases the strategy is to start a school that can be developed to the point where government will take over. The motivation is not to compete with the government system, but to be absorbed within that system. In fact, it is often explicit government policy that a community should demonstrate its interest and commitment to education by starting up its own school, which the government would then take over once certain criteria have been met.[2] In the post-independence period for many developing countries, when thousands of villages were without schools, this was probably a sensible and politically astute way of rationing limited available government resources.

A Ugandan Community School

High above the rift valley in the foothills of the Ruwenzori Mountains, lies the village of Nyakabingo. On the top of the hill stands a Catholic church and a small private school called Nyakabingo Infant Modern School. It occupies a half-built set of dusty rooms without floors and looks down on a large, well-built, fully-staffed government primary school no more than 400 metres away. The private school was started as a nursery school by the church community. The teachers are all untrained unemployed youth from the village. Gradually the school added the first and then the second year of primary school. As of 2007, it offered grade 4 and plans to offer the full cycle. Parents pay a fee for their child to attend. The teachers use English in class, even though their command of the language is weak. The pupils can manage a few words of this foreign tongue, but a whole sentence is beyond them. Nonetheless, it is enough to persuade some parents that they are getting a better education than down the road at the government school. The head teacher, a man in his twenties, has a dream that the school will one day be taken on by the government and that he might be taken for training. He could then swap his current meagre and unpredictable income for a civil servant's salary.

Religious communities and charitable societies start schools because they wish to nurture their faith, practice their vision of a better pedagogy or meet a perceived gap in government provision. In the latter case, they may be behaving in a manner similar to an entrepreneur. However, there are important distinctions to make. In most cases they are able to draw on resources (including volunteers) above and beyond those generated from pupil fees.[3] This makes it relatively easy to provide a superior service to government. Often such groups gradually exhaust their resources, their energy or their vision and ask government to take on the running of the school or provide some partial support. Such educational provision was the basis for the government-aided sector in many Organisation for Economic Co-operation and Development (OECD) countries. In Holland today most schools remain privately owned, but their funding is overwhelmingly public. In Bangladesh, the Bangladesh Rural Advance-ment Committee (BRAC) has run a massive not-for-profit system for several decades, depending largely on government partnership and the international development community for financial support. According to the 2006 annual report, there were 1.52 million children enrolled in 52,168 BRAC schools in 2005. Students do not have to pay to attend these schools.

Government contracting-out of basic education service delivery is a small but growing phe-nomenon, with countries such as Chile and the Czech Republic among the pio-neers. Of the three study countries, only India has started this practice. In some countries, the system is driven by vouchers that families use to pay for their children's education and which they can top-up from their own funds. In such countries, there may be some overlap with fee-paying, for-profit schools. In India and elsewhere, however, the more common model is that government contracts with the schools' owners (profit or not-for-profit) directly, pays the full costs of provision and children are educated free. No fees are required from the parent. The rationale driving gov-ernment sub-contracting is usually better management or more skills in responding to the needs of particular social groups.

Low-cost, for-profit education (the phenomenon of this book) is the spontaneous choice of the poor to ignore government-offered services and instead pay fees (low in rela-tive terms, but often high in respect of family income) to a private, unsubsidised entrepreneur who they believe can offer better or more cost-effective outcomes for their children.[4] None of the other four types of institution described above reflects this specific scenario, though sometimes the religious and charitable school may result in a similar dynamic.

Before leaving the issue of definition, one cannot avoid some discussion of the term 'low cost'. This is a relative term, which brings imprecision into the definition. Each country study explains what this means in the specific national context. In general terms, the definition is more straightforward than it may appear at first. In the rural context, 'low cost' indicates that most of the enrolment is from a typical village and its satellites. A high-cost school in a rural setting, by contrast, would normally have a very wide catchment (tens or hundreds of kilometres), where children are brought from a great distance by their guardians or the school, using motorised means. They would be kept in a boarding environment, and only a handful of children at most from the neighbouring villages would be enrolled as fee-paying students.

Defining 'low cost' in an urban setting is less clear-cut, but can be related to some of the same factors. The location of the low-cost school would be in a poor ward or slum. Enrolment would be from the local community. Children would all be day students, mostly travelling from home to school by foot. Most parents would be renting their homes and would travel to work by foot or public transport.

Each of the country studies has tried to examine the applicability of the definition in its own context, and to understand the role of non-profit or high-cost non-government providers, but the case studies and the bulk of the analytical effort have been devoted to the low-cost commercial sector. It is hoped that by so doing, the book will be more focused and more useful in raising pertinent policy issues.

Study methodology

Quantifying the phenomenon

The first challenge of any study into private schooling in developing countries is the lack of data. Many or even the majority of low-cost private schools may not be registered. The incentives for registration may be few and the costs of the registration process, both formal and informal, may be very high. Even if government is aware of the schools and is able to deliver the census form to them, there may be suspicion and reluctance on the part of the owners about supplying information.[5]

The obvious problem is that the information obtained from routine sources may be very partial and underestimate the extent of the phenomenon. The study attempted to overcome this problem by triangulating information from several sources. EMIS data was examined and EMIS staff were asked about private school response rates and estimations of under-counting. Also, where available, the country consultants reviewed special studies undertaken on private schools for comparison with EMIS data nationally or on a sub-national sample basis.

A second problem with measurement arises from identifying subcategories of non-government schools. The EMIS systems for the three countries do not use the same sub-definition of non-government schools:

- India: the District Information System for Education (DISE) is the national EMIS. It includes many private, unaided schools and other categories such as open schools and other kinds of informal provision.

- Nigeria: only two categories are recognised by the Nigeria EMIS (government and private). A large number of schools are ignored if government deems them to fail minimum standards.

- Uganda: there are three categories of education institution based on ownership (government, community and private). The national EMIS does not distinguish between types of private schools. District registers are very partial, but they do sometimes record additional information regarding private schools. This may include the school's religious foundation, whether it is a commercial enterprise, if the registration fee is paid up-to-date, whether the school has submitted an EMIS return and details of any inspections.

The problem is exacerbated by the following difficulties:

- Is each subcategory equally under-reported? Generally, the low-cost subcategories are unreported because the incentive is to avoid officialdom (bribes, fines and labour laws).

- The patterns are not generally consistent across each country because different histories have given rise to different developments on the ground. For example, Tanzania's Kilimanjaro region has the largest number of secondary schools in the country: 57 governmental and 74 non-governmental. This is because Christian missionaries established the first formal schools in this region and the tradition of non-government education still persists.[6] In Nigeria, the distribution of Qur'anic schools varies from state to state based on religion and history.

Perhaps the only reliable way of obtaining data on this phenomenon would be through a national household survey, such as the Demographic and Health Survey (DHS). A DHS for education data has been completed for both Uganda and Nigeria.[7] These surveys detail the distribution of pupils across government, private religious and private non-religious schools, as well as statistics on proximity to school. In addition to this, the DHS often includes questions about household members' schooling, such as current enrolment, distance to school, reasons for not attending school and highest educational attainment of each household member. This could be supplemented by asking about the ownership and management of schools where children are currently enrolled.

Conducting a nationally-valid survey such as the DHS is very expensive and was beyond the resources of this research, but one of the research conclusions is that national authorities need to add such questions/analysis in future to existing national surveys in order to better quantify and track this phenomenon. For example, in Nigeria the reasons given for school choice are not disaggregated by school type, nor are the reasons for dropping out, attendance etc. In these examples the data is available, but the analysis is absent. In India, it is common for a child to register in both the government school and the private school. Registration in a government school entitles the pupil to a midday meal, amongst other things, but the pupil actually attends class at the private school. Also, the distinction of whether a school is registered or unregistered is absent in the national statistics in the three country studies. This information is very important. The phenomenon of unregistered schools is impossible to measure if surveys fail to distinguish between the two types.

Taking into account the various problems discussed above, the aim of the study methodology was to construct an accurate picture of the under-reporting of low-cost private schools in the case study locations through three independent methods. First, the country consultants were to gain access to EMIS data and interrogate it to assess what details were available on low-cost private schools. Secondly, they would compare this data with information gathered from local officials, representatives of teachers unions and school proprietors in the area. Thirdly, the country consultants were to undertake a rapid tour of the area to verify for themselves the number of low-cost private schools to be found there. The Nigerian study came closest to achieving this aim. The numbers in India turned out to be too vast for the consultant to be able to conduct a complete quantified survey, while the Uganda sample was not representative of the southern districts where the majority of private low-cost schools occur.

The context: historically, politically and socially

The development of a country's education system is inevitably an emotive and highly political process. Local societal and historical factors must be taken into account when implementing policy to ensure that reforms do not have unintended consequences. In Uganda, education was divided on racial lines before the country gained its independence, a system that fomented and institutionalised differences and inequality in the population. In Nigeria, partnerships between the colonial education system and missionary societies were perceived to have an agenda to change the religious balance within society. Today, the introduction of universal free primary education across the developing world may well give rise to a mushrooming of private schools if governments allow per-pupil spending to collapse. If private extra tuition has become the norm in government schools, then there may be little or no actual saving in sending children to a supposedly free government school as opposed to a low-cost private school.

In order to explore the historical, political, social, regulatory and legal frameworks, the country teams undertook a series of interviews with key informants at the national level and focus groups at the local level. The interviewees were selected from policy-makers, front line education administrators, school inspectors, private school owners and teachers' unions.

The institutional and family dynamics: case study purpose

The researchers tried to obtain the views and beliefs regarding the dynamics of decision-making by private school entrepreneurs, their parent customers and local government schools. Thus the country case studies looked at communities where there was a clear choice between one or more government schools and a low-cost private school. The key informants in each community were taken from both a government and a private school.

The focus group discussions explored a range of issues and were deliberately open in format to allow all types of issues to be raised. Key issues which featured consistently included:

- Factors of parental choice between school type;

- Relative perceptions of quality (strengths and weaknesses);

- Relative perceptions of safety for pupils;

- Curriculum variations between schools;

- Differential delivery strategies (school day, flexible terms, subject coverage, time on task etc.);

- Governance issues, including participation of parents in school decision-making, and transparency issues, such as the access to information and independent checking systems;

- Actual costs and total household costs per student;

- Monitoring, quality control and performance improvement strategies; and

- Differential decision-making by gender of child.

Notes

1. The situation in India is that the majority of private schools are de facto commercial enterprises, but taxation law forces most owners to create a foundation. A small number of pupils usually benefit from the owners' largesse. See Tooley, J. [2005a].

2. Tanzania in the immediate post-independence period required communities to construct school buildings before government could take on the running of a school (Chediel, Sekwao & Kirumba [2000]); the Kenyan *harambee* system launched by Kenyatta used similar principles, as did Numeri's '*El Auwn el Zati*' in Sudan. Currently in Zambia, the community schools initiative, which enjoys wide donor support, is meant to be a part of the government-supported (part-funded) system (De Stefano, J. [2006]).

3. 'Religious organisations have access to resources that can serve to subsidize the expenses of schooling' Belfield, C. & Levin, H.M. (2002).

4. Tooley (2005a) found that the majority of unaided private school in Hyderabad and Lagos were of the type that this study is looking at, i.e. low-cost, for-profit schools.

5. In most low-income countries, each school is sent a form in advance of the annual school census period, which is then filled and returned to the authorities. This is the system upon which most education management information systems are based before schools can be enrolled into fully-integrated IT-based management information systems, like those in OECD countries which cost over $2,000 per school per annum (UK commercial price quote).

6. Chediel, Sekao and Kirumba (2000).

7. The next DHS Education Data survey is due in 2009. Donors (the World Bank and the UK Department for International Development, DFID) are committed to help states to 'understand and regulate the private sector and develop Public Private Partnerships'.

3

The International Context

Private schools and the impact of under-reporting

Low-cost private schools represent a sub-sector in the shadows. An often uncomfortable relationship with the authorities means that many schools operate without registration and fail to report their data.

The treatment of unrecognised and low-cost private schools is a major dilemma. The United Nations Educational, Scientific and Cultural Organization (UNESCO) Institution for Statistics (UIS) urged caution when attempting to survey such institutions, 'as they may not meet the requirement of UPE as regards of quality education... data provided to UIS typically do not cover those schools.'[1] All three countries have data gaps.

In India, 'different data sources tell different story.'[2] It is widely reported across the country that there is a 'large-scale dual enrolment, whereby children draw entitlements from the government school while actually studying in the private schools.'[3] A recent study in Punjab found that if enrolment in unrecognised schools was taken into account, the gross enrolment rate (GER) in the area would be 26 per cent higher.[4] The DISE 2005–06 data on private schools shows that they comprise 16.9 per cent of total schools and unaided private are 11.2 per cent of the total. The situation is confused; official statistics show age-specific enrolment above 100 per cent, but field observations in the various studies estimate that between 5 per cent and 40 per cent of children attend unrecognised schools.[5] The EFA Global Monitoring Report 2008 puts the number of out-of-school children in India in 2005 at 6.395 million, second only to Nigeria. It possible that a sizeable number of children are 'hidden' in unrecognised schools, which their parents believe will offer better life chances than the government system.

According to the EFA Global Monitoring Report 2008, Nigeria has 6.584 million children out of school. The proportion of children enrolled in private schools has increased from 4.6 per cent to 7.2 per cent in recent years, but there are still claims of significant under-reporting in some states. 'In Kano, there are currently 3.0 million children enrolled in 28,000 Islamiyya and Qur'anic, as compared with nearly 4,000 public and private schools catering for over 1.5 million children.'[6] The data analysis and entry in respect of the national census 2006 was still going on at the time of writing. This will shed some comparative light in gross and net enrolments (a GER of 103 per cent and a net enrolment ratio (NER) of 68 per cent in 2005 are reported in the EFA 2008 report). The planned Nigeria Education Household Survey in 2009 can disaggregate enrolment by school type and registration status as well as numerous indictors.

The Ministry of Education and Sports (MoES) in Uganda acknowledges that coverage of private institutions is not complete and data is inconsistent from year to year. Private institutions are reluctant to provide data to the government. The study of unregistered, low-cost private schools is relatively new. This study found little information. In 15 of 19 northern districts, researchers were able to assess the number of private schools. The study's estimate of 90 private schools compares to the MoES official list, which only includes 34. Anecdotal reports claim that the mushrooming of low-cost private schools has grown fastest in Greater Kampala and next fastest in Uganda's central region. The country's GER was 119 per cent in 2005, although the NER is not reported in the EFA 2008 report. Uganda needs to estimate the underreporting of private schools, starting in Greater Kampala and proceeding to an appropriate set of questions in the DHS.

Stability of the market niche

The mushrooming of private schools signals a very rapid response to market opportunity.[7] Some of the factors that have given rise to such opportunity are highly context-specific. Some of the most important factors are:

- An over-supply of teachers;
- High hidden costs of government schooling;
- Private tuition costs;
- Language of instruction; and
- Poor performance of the public sector.

Teacher supply

Where a country has produced a large number of teachers in excess of the needs of the public sector, this can create a supply-side factor promoting private education. The surplus teachers are eager to work for private school owners, especially where alternative opportunities for employment in the non-agricultural sectors of the economy are limited. With few alternatives, they are often ready to accept wages well below government teacher rates. Sometimes those higher government rates can encourage them to stay within the teaching profession working for 'apprentice'-level wages, waiting for openings in the unionised and pensionable government sector. The prospect of high and dependable earnings later in their career can make the low and unpredictable payments of the private school tolerable.[8] Teachers' pay is typically the largest single portion of a school's costs. At present in Ugandan private schools, teachers earn 61 per cent less than in government schools. Closing this gap even to 50 per cent would mean an increase in total cost to the private school owner of 33 per cent. The private owner is constrained by the market to pass over the cost increase. The only options available to the owner would be to increase the fees or to cut costs somehow, for example by reducing the purchase of textbooks.

The surplus supply of teachers in Uganda is a result of government teacher training policy. The surplus will only be maintained if governments continue to train more teachers than are required by the public sector for expansion and replacement of attrition. Government may take on additional teachers to reduce teacher-pupil ratios if public finances allow – thereby reducing the surplus available to the private sector. Government might also decide to close government teacher training colleges to reduce the surplus.[9] In many countries, government is the overwhelming supplier of primary schoolteachers (in Uganda, only 4 per cent of teacher trainees attend non-government colleges). Overall there is a large current surplus that enables the private sector to offer low-cost education. This, however, may be a temporary phenomenon.

India, on the other hand, has produced a large number of secondary and university graduates in the cities and villages waiting for an opportunity of a job or a further chance of training or education. The majority are not trained teachers, but school owners and parents deem them suitable to be teachers, especially if they are more dedicated than government teachers.

Hidden costs of government schools

In many countries, including the three in this book, education is declared to be free. In reality, however, there may be hidden costs that are substantial enough to change the balance of benefits between a government and private school in favour of the latter, despite its fees. Such costs vary from one situation to another, but typically may include:

- The cost of transport/travel if a private school is much closer to a child's home;

- The costs of ancillary items at the government school, such as uniforms, pencils, books and other school materials, local 'donations' to school maintenance and development and additional paid lessons for certain classes;[10] and

- The opportunity cost of a child's labour if the government school takes them away from home for a substantially longer period than the private school.

In extreme cases, such as in elite government secondary schools in Uganda, a school may be owned or supported by the state, but its services are virtually private because parents pay the bulk of the costs required to deliver the education services.

For parents choosing between the local government primary school and the local low-cost private school, it must be assumed that they consider the cost of each in total; where the difference between the two is not substantial, this must increase demand for the private school. Here is another situation where government policy could easily change the arithmetic of choice. As governments become richer, they traditionally take on a more comprehensive set of responsibilities for school costs, such as pens, materials, feeding (from 2003, Indian states have been bound to provide a midday meal scheme), transport to school etc. This may reduce the competitiveness of the low-cost private sector.

Private tuition

Belfield and Levin quote seven East Asian countries where the costs of private tutoring 'constitute a large proportion of total expenditures [on education]'.[11] There are examples in other parts of the world, such as Egypt in the Middle East.[12]

The impact is similar to the hidden costs of government schools. If one has to pay for private tutoring in addition to the government school, then it is this total cost which must be compared with the alternative private school.[13]

Private tutoring by teachers on the state payroll is often banned by government on the grounds that it encourages teachers to reserve 'real learning' for their private lessons, and because it extends the school day beyond that which is reasonable for the child. However, in this case it seems that governments find the phenomenon hard to control.[14] Perhaps this practice may be less susceptible to government action than other factors discussed.

The situation in this respect seems to be different in each country. In Nigeria, private tuition is not widespread. In contrast, unofficial tuition payments are widespread in Uganda government schools, but private schools do not practise it. Interestingly, urban parents in Egypt pay heavily for their children's private tuition, regardless of whether they are enrolled in government or private schools.

Language of instruction

A common determinant of school choice in each of the three country studies was the use of English as the language of instruction in the private school, or its greater prominence as compared with the government curriculum. From the parental perspective, English competence is a decisive skill in the modern labour market, offering the prospect of white-collar employment for their children. Intuitively they believe that an early start to this language will enhance their children's future. The academic evidence points to the opposite being true.[15]

If this is a critical factor in parental choice, then it is also a fragile niche for the private sector because it is actually commonly illegal. Many countries require even private schools to use a common curriculum as a means of ensuring social cohesion and pedagogical soundness. Conversely, there are countries such as Holland that grant the freedom to choose one's educational system as part of their constitution, but these are generally the exception to the rule.

Here, the vulnerability of the private sector relation is that curriculum change is outside its control. Government could impose a standard curriculum on all schools, or it could move the curriculum of government schools closer to the type offered in private schools. Examples of the latter are frequent. Several countries such as Yemen and Egypt have decided to introduce English at a lower grade than had previously been the case, and some countries such as Palestine have decided to start teaching it as a subject from grade 1.[16] In each of the study countries, the parental preference of English is one of the leading reasons for choosing a private education. In Indian government schools, English is not introduced at the infant level. Parents claim that the standard of English teaching is better in the private sector. The new primary curriculum introduced in India in 2007 is attracting a lot of criticism from parents. Some parents cite it as one of the main reasons to choose a private school.

Low quality in the public sector

Another major driving force behind demand for private education is perceived failings in the public school system. Common issues include:

- Teacher absenteeism and low morale;

- Rigidities of a centralised management system that leave schools without even minimal operational costs and unable to make important decisions;

- Lack of professional support and in-service training for teachers;

- Irregular or corrupt inspection services; and

- Political patronage as a factor behind weak school management.

Often the public sector is capable of very significant improvements when it seeks to address the above factors. One technique being employed around the world is the devolution of resources and accountability to the school level. This promises significant gains in effectiveness. The World Development Report 2004 (World Bank) entitled 'Making Services Work for Poor People' discusses this subject:

> 'Increasing poor clients' choice and participation in service delivery will help them monitor and discipline providers. Raising poor citizens' voice, through the ballot box and widely available information, can increase their influence with policymakers – and reduce the diversion of public services to the non-poor for political patronage. By rewarding the effective delivery of services and penalising the ineffective, policymakers can get providers to serve poor people better.'

Furthermore, the World Bank Independent Evaluation Group writing in 2006: 'Support for local government and school management of primary education has been more effective than support for central government'.[17] This is particularly the case when devolution is coupled with regular in-service training to build local capacity.

However, in the majority of poor countries, government schools are perceived to be beset by inherited inefficiencies and poor management.

Entrepreneurial response

There are several questions that need to be asked in considering the future impact of low-cost private schools in developing countries.

First, what is the likelihood of significant change in some of the key factors just described: teacher supply; hidden costs and quality of government schooling; curriculum and private tuition? And secondly, what is the likely reaction of low-cost private school owners to such changes?

The impact of universal primary education in Uganda in 1996 was dramatic. There was a mass evacuation from private schools, which were well established in the larger villages in central Uganda. When some months later it became apparent that government-promised inputs were not forthcoming, many parents moved their children back to private schools. A large group of commentators blame this for the growth and expansion of private schools to all parts of country, which had not witnessed the phenomenon before. India and Nigeria have not experienced such a dramatic dip in demand.

The reaction of the low-cost private school owners is hard to predict, because in the three country studies the sub-sector has not yet faced any constraints on growth. In theory, the response to such shocks as heavier regulation or an increase in costs will depend on a variety of factors:

- Mobility of the capital and human resources deployed in the private schools – Can facilities be redeployed for alternative use? Were investors drawn to education purely by the rate of return, or because there were teachers lacking alternative employment? The more mobile the capital, the more likely it is to be quickly redeployed according to the shifting economic of education. However, if the capital is relatively immobile, then there will be a greater tendency for owners to try to adapt their product to the changing market place.

- Demand elasticity. This will be very high if the private schools' customers perceive private schools and government schools to be almost the same product differentiated by current price and quality. A small increase in the price of private school fees would result in a large reduction on demand. On the other hand, if private schooling is viewed as intrinsically better because of perceived superiority of private provision or because the village elite all send their children to the school, then the aspirational nature of education may lead parents to do their utmost to meet fee increases despite hardships.

Many low-cost private schools are run in the owner's house or shop. The conversion of premises is not usually an expensive matter. If the market for primary schools is depressed, it is a simple matter to re-open as a nursery, secondary or technical institute. If the whole education sector is depressed, the owner could let the rooms to poor families.

In the short to medium term, one would expect the private sector to respond to increasing competition from the public sector with a mixture of price increases, innovation and efficiency gains, as well as some reduction in the number of suppliers. Longer-term major shifts in the economics of educational provision are likely to reduce the number of new entrants and bring about consolidation among those who are most efficient and effective in meeting parental aspirations.

If this is the general trend, one might expect a long-term future for private schools, which sees them gradually move up-market and increase fees to meet the aspirational expectations of their customers in parallel to gradual improvement of the government sector. The result would be a more traditional elite focus of the private school sector.

Possible impacts/options for the low-cost private sector

The last section looked at growth of the low-cost private sector as a spontaneous phenomenon, often outside government control and not yet incorporated into any proactive government policy. In the majority of cases, the policy-makers in the study countries ignore the potential to constructively engage with unregistered schools. The Educational Quality Improvement Programme (EQUIP) in Uttar Pradesh presents an exception to this, and has been bringing about quality improvement in hundreds of low-cost schools. It is possible that as low-cost private schools become more visible, policy-makers' attitudes could change towards constructive engagement. India has a lot of experience with a multiplicity of models in the formal and informal school/learning sectors.

In Nigeria and Uganda there are many options for government to actively engage with the private sector, which could play a more deliberate and constructive role in accomplishing national education objectives. In such a vision, the private sector's niche is seen as important and its expansion potentially desirable. In Africa, there has been little exploration of the role of the private school sector as service provider. A weak governance track record makes the owners suspicious of inference, while other weaknesses in economics, planning and financial modelling and budgeting have made it difficult to introduce promising reforms.

One last footnote is remarkable. In India, 37 per cent of government schoolteachers with children are choosing to send them to private schools.[18] This represents a damning loss of confidence in public schools.

Criteria for assessing the value of the private sector to education development

Belfield and Levin (2002) propose four basic criteria for evaluating a reform that promotes privatisation in education. These criteria ask:

- 'Will the reform give freedom of choice to those demanding education?'

- 'Will the reform be efficient?' (by providing more outputs per $1 or providing the same output more cheaply)

- 'Will the reform be equitable ... to students and communities?'

- 'Will the reform generate the social cohesion that an education system is expected to contribute to an effectively functioning society with common values and institutions?'

The remaining sections of this chapter look at each of these issues in turn. In the context of the first issue, freedom of choice, we also look at the impact of low-cost private schools on governance and accountability to parents.

Issues of freedom of choice

It is generally argued and is supported by the studies (the Nigeria study being the most thorough in terms of documenting) that parents appreciate the opportunity to choose their child's school.[19] This factor increases levels of satisfaction and it is assumed that it acts as a spur to the performance of all schools involved in this quasi competition.

The low-cost private school phenomenon does seem to be very closely linked to parental desire for choice. Interviews with study schools reveal that parents value such choice as a way to select a service which is different from that offered by the government school. The nature of that difference varies according to the school and individual parental perception. Characteristics that are frequently highlighted include:

- Different curriculum choices, especially in respect to the language of instruction and sometimes additional subjects (e.g. Qur'anic schools in Nigeria). The importance of English in the three study countries is crucial. In India, many low-cost private schools claim to be an 'English Medium School'. However, like peri-urban schools in Uganda, the English language competence of the teachers leaves a lot be desired.

- A more convenient timetable, school day or calendar is sometimes mentioned. The owner normally sets these things at the convenience of the parents.

- Higher quality of the learning is often described in terms of factors such as teacher commitment. It is problematic to describe the norms of the low-cost private schools as 'higher' quality. Equipment and furniture are generally less than in government schools. Provision of textbooks by government is also more generous compared with unregistered schools in each of the three countries. However, parents all agree that the low-cost private school beats the government school in all aspects of discipline, punctual attendance by teachers and pupils, politeness, time on tasks, control of bullying etc.

- A safer environment if the school is closer to home, run by trusted persons or staff of similar religious beliefs. In north Nigeria, this factor is very important for girls and makes the private Qur'anic school attractive to parents.

- There is greater perceived accountability of staff, who depend for their salaries on parental payment of fees. Staff also lack any employment protection: in most cases the owner is judge, jury and executioner should there be a dispute.

At first sight it would seem intrinsically beneficial to have greater choice. However, there are potential dangers. Some parents might choose to give their children less than an optimal amount of education. In the United States, for example, parents are allowed to opt for home schooling if they feel that better fits their cultural and social needs. Other countries might feel that this is too difficult to control and may therefore risk some parents simply exploiting their children's labour at home or in the family business. Low-cost private schools that compete with government schools could attract parents who want to reduce school time, especially if the real costs of the two options are not decisively in favour of the government school.[20]

It may also be dangerous to assume that parents make the right choices when offered alternative pedagogical approaches. The choice of English language instruction, as discussed above, is an example where parents may be making a poor choice. It may appear to work in the short term (children managing a few words of English), but leads to failure in the long term when basic language skills are missing. Schools that only teach a religious curriculum might be omitting core skills required by all children.[21] Some schools might insist on omitting certain topics that they found distasteful, such as HIV/AIDS prevention messages or discussion of a historical conflict in which the ethnic group enrolled were accepted to have committed atrocities.

All of these potential problems are controllable if the private sector is subject to regulation and quality control. While in theory there is no reason why government cannot institute such a regime, it is often beyond the government's capacity in a developing country, where governance systems may be weak. It may be impossible to institute a fair and efficient system of government school inspection, for example. So it may similarly be impossible to maintain an incorruptible regulatory system for the private schools. In the case study countries there are examples of supportive district

---

Held Back

One mother in Kampala, with only four years of primary education herself but with great ambitions for her children, described to the researcher how she wanted her children to be properly prepared for the competitive environment of primary school. So she made her son repeat the final year of private kindergarten three times until he was proficient in repetition of the English alphabet. As a result, the boy did not start primary school until he was eight years old (two years behind schedule) and gained a skill that many educators would consider pedagogically unsound, especially for kindergarten. However, the mother was convinced she was doing the best for her son.

---

officials arranging in-service training, but there are also examples of greedy administrators exhorting school owners to make un-receipted payments to individuals.

The issue of accountability is closely related to the issue of quality. Is a private school more accountable than a public school just because parents are paying fees? This is a very doubtful proposition. True accountability arises from participation in the definition of a school's objectives and targets, and sharing of objective performance data. A private school may offer parents only one means of signalling dissatisfaction: the withdrawal of their child from the school. In the absence of effective independent inspection, the parent may receive little objective information on school quality. There may be, in effect, no consumer protection. Parental withdrawal of a child from a school is a major decision and can have negative impact on the child's development. A school is not a corner shop where you can choose on daily basis which rival offers the best prices and quality.

The issues of accountability and governance are especially serious where parental literacy is low and access to knowledge regarding good pedagogical practice is limited. This may be another area where government should consider regulation of the private sector, to ensure parents have a voice in the educational process and are guaranteed access to critical performance information. The evidence of the studies is mixed. Some owners are ready to welcome parental participation, but some are secretive and resist discussing management information. Parents need their rights to be protected by the law and a regulatory regime that is just and equitable.

Issues of efficiency

There are two main ways in which low-cost private schools could improve the overall efficiency of the education system. The first is by providing additional education capacity for a society with little or no requirement for public investment. The second is by improving efficiency through competitive pressure.

Potential for increasing capacity of the system with minimal investment

Society can benefit from private sector school capacity in a variety of ways:

- At the simplest level, government is relieved of the burden of paying for children whose parents choose to purchase private instead of government service provision. The saving is obviously equal to the per child public subsidy.

- Government can purchase places in private schools. The government motivation may derive from many sources: efficiency, reform, pro-poor choice etc., but the essential rationale is to increase capacity.[22]

Two of the study countries are funding the private sector to educate some part of the population. India has funded aided private schools to deliver education services since the 1970s, and such schools receive the bulk of their funding, including salaries, from the government. In subsequent years, the government has added categories such as non-formal education and working children, with special arrangements for each type. Even unregistered schools have managed to obtain scholarship money from the government.[23] Uganda offered a subsidy for private schools in the early days of UPE, but the planning and control systems were weak and the schemes were gradually abandoned. Upon the introduction of universal secondary education, such schemes were tried again. The government has contracted low-cost private secondary schools to utilise their spare private capacity in areas where government school places are insufficient. Examples of the government funding the private sector are, in truth, many; Belfield and Levin (2002) quote examples from every continent including the Dominican Republic, Chile and Czech Republic.

Though attractive in principle, implementation of such schemes may be quite complex. Issues that need to be considered include:

- Who is to assess the capacity of the private school and against what criteria and standards? In other words, how is the capacity of school defined? Is the school simply a place or a learning opportunity of a defined quality?

- Which children would be eligible and what impact might different selection systems have on existing clients for the private school? They might be tempted to try to gain free entry through a government scholarship, in which case government would be assuming an additional burden rather than buying an additional place.

- If exclusivity and social advantage are major motivators for parental choice of the private sector, what impact would there be on that demand if a school accepted additional students from a social cross section supported by government scholarship? What impact might this have on the social mix in government schools in the neighbourhood?[24]

- What quality control processes would be necessary to ensure that government received value for money for its scholarship? Some owners might be tempted to accept additional funding without increasing inputs, leading to a reduction in quality of service?

- What opportunities are there for misdirection or misuse of resources by officials or beneficiaries?

The private sector's role in making new investments in education is an idea with which a number of Organization of Petroleum Exporting Countries (OPEC) and OECD countries are experimenting. However, the whole topic of private-public partnership investments is complex and is likely to prove itself in traditional sectors such as roads, power etc. rather than schools.[25]

Potential for improving efficiency through competition

Generally speaking, competition is considered to lead to improved quality as service providers respond to market demand. However, the extent to which there is real competition may be limited by many factors:

- Parental choice may be limited by distance from schools and transport in many poor rural communities. The population density is 345 (population per square kilometre) in India (2005), 153 in Nigeria (2005) and 120 in Uganda (2005).[26] The opportunity for competition should be plentiful in many parts of all three countries. The India study shows competition to be commonplace, with entrepreneurs opening schools right next to government schools. However, is the competition healthy or 'beggar-my-neighbour', leaving all parties weaker? Some parts of India are experiencing declining school rolls.

- Innovation may be limited by government regulation, because of concern to maintain standards or to ensure social cohesion or because of simple inertia, so that the areas of discretion left to schools may be limited.

- In order for competition from a private school to have a positive impact on a neighbouring government school, there has to be some incentive for the latter to respond (such as increased income when additional students are enrolled) or a penalty (such as the threat of closure if enrolment were to drop severely). Such pressure might be strong in a government system with school-based management and funding linked primarily to enrolment. In all the study countries, however, most management decision-making takes place in the bureaucracy at the district or state level, and funding is slow to respond to changes in enrolment.

- It may be that a certain scale and certainty regarding the rules of the new game are needed to create a major competitive impact on the education system. Parents, entrepreneurs and government school managers are not going to take radical decisions unless they believe there is a long-term commitment to change by the government. That is a tough challenge for many governments in a very politically-sensitive area.

- It should also be noted that competition can be created even within the public sector by creating a quasi market and facilitating inter-community transport. This has been a growing trend in the UK.

The reader must bear in mind the situation of the country studies. The role of competition and choice is based on the total cost for poor families. Most parents may simply be choosing the cheapest of two low-quality products, with price being the overriding consideration.

Issues of equity

Low-cost private schooling is very different from the high-cost elite education that almost guarantees its buyers a place for their children in the best universities and top jobs. The first question in considering issues of equity is whether low-cost schools are actually delivering a better product?

The evidence is not easy to analyse. There are many difficulties in using examination results. For example, the candidates from unregistered private schools usually sit as candidates in a nearby government or private registered school. Ideally the researcher needs standardised tests to be able to make a fair comparison. Such tests are not often carried out in unregistered private schools.

Tooley (2005a) cites results of standardised tests in Ghana, India and Lagos, Nigeria. The mean scores for English and mathematics in private schools were uniformly better than government schools. Furthermore, the registered private schools did better across the board than their unregistered counterparts. The table below illustrates the percentage points by which registered and unregistered private schools outperformed the government schools in each of the locations.

With the exception of his evidence from Kenya, which is not displayed here, Tooley demonstrated a higher level of performance in the private sector. The testing in Kenya was happening in the throws of a UPE transformation when children were moving from one school to another.

Is there any evidence of social partitioning or ethnic separation? The latter might arise in some environments, because of language issues in a mixed-language society. No evidence of social partitioning based on ethnic and caste division is provided in the studies. Anecdotal evidence is widespread that private education is creating division based on wealth, albeit private education in Nigeria and India are available to suit all budgets.

If private schools are leading to social partitioning, vouchers can be used to reduce this phenomenon as they can guarantee access for all social classes. The India scholarships system is intended to redress inequalities by the value of scholarships. A system of vouchers is unlikely to be effective in poor countries with weak government, however. Unless a country reaches a level of gross domestic product (GDP)

Table 3.1 Private schools' out-performance on government schools

Percentage points out-performance on government schools	Mathematics		English	
	Unregistered private	Registered private	Unregistered private	Registered private
Hyderabad, India	22%	25%	31%	37%
Ghana	6%	12%	9%	14%
Lagos, Nigeria	15%	19%	23%	30%

that enables serious consideration of social safety nets (i.e. middle income), vouchers are likely to prove disappointing.

Equity is a genuine concern of many observers. An education officer in Nigeria laments the evacuation of the middle classes from government schools in Lagos. Meanwhile, a common attitude among teachers in India is that having never had any access to education, the poor should be grateful that they are now able to access the 'favour' of free government education.

It is not reasonable to blame the parents. They naturally seek any possible special advantage in a climate of brutal social competition. All three education systems are being driven by high-stakes examinations, and the private schools do claim better performance over public schools.

Issues of social cohesion

Education can serve to level the differences and inequalities between children from varying social classes or races. Conversely, limiting admission to pupils on the grounds of their family's financial means can serve to reinforce existing inequalities. This can have a further impact upon social cohesion, which may be endangered if the education system exacerbates a society's fault lines and lays the seeds of conflict, instead of creating a citizenry with shared values, mutual understanding and obligations.

The flip side of choice is the danger of disunity. The extent to which this is problematic clearly depends on the degree to which a society is homogeneous and relatively egalitarian. The danger may be minimal in a small rich northern European country, and critical in a weak multilingual African country recovering from civil war.

Nonetheless, growth of private schooling is not synonymous with the phenomenon described above. The use of a common core curriculum, fundamental enforced rights of access to any school by all social groups, the banning of material designed to incite racial or ethnic hatred, the promotion of peace studies and civic education, together with strong enforcement of regulation are all more important in fighting social conflict than the ownership of the schools.

Successive governments in Uganda tried to weaken the linkage between churches and education. They feared that this acerbated the sectarian divisions in society. Many Arab countries have preferred to suppress confessional education out of fear of sectarianism. However, India and Nigeria seem relaxed about the impact of private schools and a variety of school choices.

Notes

1. UNESCO Institute for Statistics, email correspondence July 2007.
2. Ibid, p. 2.

3. See section 4.2.3 The emergence of the inexpensive schools.

4. Mehta, A. (2005).

5. Aggarwal, Y. (2000) and Muralidharan, K. & Kremer, M. (2006).

6. Adediran, S. (2007).

7. The World Bank's evaluation of support to primary education cites Mali, Ghana, India and Pakistan as examples of growth in low-cost secular private schools. See World Bank (2006).

8. Smith, I. & Musoke, S. (2006).

9. In both Uganda and Malawi, government has been trying to reduce the surplus of teachers to some extent.

10. Uniforms are often sold by school management as a monopoly and a form of hidden fees. Donations are often compulsory, with heavy social pressure to meet obligations regardless of family means. Additional paid classes are common for examination classes, where the system has a high-stakes terminal examination that determines future options for secondary schooling.

11. Belfield & Levin (2002).

12. Bray, M. (1999).

13. This assumes that enrolment in the private school removes the necessity of private tutoring. This is the case in some countries in some circumstances, but in Egypt it has become the norm for private tutoring in the cities to encompass children from both the private and public sectors.

14. It is difficult to control because it usually takes place off school premises. It may also be driven as much by parental concern for children's performance in a highly competitive job market with little or no social safety net, as by teacher's manipulation of their in-school programmes.

15. The evidence from comparative research is overwhelming that all language skills, including second language proficiency, are enhanced by mother tongue instruction in infant years. See Komarek, K. (2003) and Center for Applied Linguistics (2004).

16. Nicolai, S. (2005).

17. World Bank (2006).

18. Muralidharan, K. & Kremer, M. (2006).

19. Belfield & Levin (2003): parents want 'differentiated demand' from that offered by the state; parents want more ('excess demand'); and there is much economic evidence that monetary returns have risen over the period since 1990.

20. Nonetheless, some evidence from De Stefano (2006) shows that rural elite parents actually value longer school on the assumption that it improves competitiveness of pupils in final exams; more time at school might be preferred in urban areas because parents value the childminding function (Bray [1999]). This factor is highly context-specific.

21. Some commentators emphasise bad cases in Mali, Ivory Coast and West African countries in Qur'anic schools where itinerant teachers refuse non-traditional subjects and exploit children (United Nations Office for the Coordination of Humanitarian Affairs [2007]).

22. The government may purchase places in the private system, thereby saving investment resources which would otherwise have been needed to create that capacity in the

government system. In assessing the value of this arrangement, the government needs to take into account the discounted value of this saving in investment and set it off against the per pupil cost in the private system versus what it would have cost them in the public system.

23. Tilak, J.B.G. (2004): pp. 343–59, calculates 'More than one-fifth of the government expenditure on elementary (primary and upper primary) goes in the form of subsidies to private schools.'

24. Evidence from OECD countries suggests that schools need a balanced social mix in order to perform optimally.

25. In 'Breaking the State Monopoly in the Provision of Schooling' (2005) McIntosh, N. discusses the potential investment of private capital in education.

26. UN Population Division (2006).

4
INDIA
Subir Shukla and Priti Joshi

Introduction

School types in India and low-cost private education

As commercial institutions that derive profit from providing education to a non-elite clientele, private schools have a history of more than two decades in India. In the 1970s, fees were abolished in government schools and public funding extended to a section of private schools, which came to be known as 'aided' schools. 'Unaided' private schools raise their own revenues through fees and fall in two categories – recognised (or complying with a number of conditions) and unrecognised. Recognition entitles schools to issue terminal grade completion certificates and certain government provisions, including scholarships.

Both recognised and unrecognised schools are accessed by the poor. It is the numbers of latter that has grown the most. These schools are distinct from other categories, such as schools set up by philanthropic organisations, NGOs and faith-based organisations; they rely solely on the fees collected and their functioning is governed by market mechanisms rather than ideological or religious disposition. Their rapid growth in a country where government schools offer free education (and other incentives) is as much due to their entrepreneurial efforts as the self-evident dysfunctional nature of the government schools.

From the 1990s, the Government of India launched large-scale primary and elementary education programmes that focused on generating demand and increasing provision. The result was a dramatic increase in the school-going population, but also parental dissatisfaction at the quality of government schools (though in some parts of the country there were also innovative and effective government efforts). Local entrepreneurs capitalised on this and began offering a competing, low-cost product/service. A sizeable section continued to be enrolled in both the government and private schools, using one for entitlements (such as midday meals or uniform) and the other for education. Though widely reported, data on this is unfortunately not available.

Since such a great range is available, the study looks at the following low-fee private schools:

• Those used by the poorest, fee-paying population in any area; and

- Those charging a monthly fee roughly equivalent to a little over two days' earning for a typical daily wage worker of the area.

Tracking the scale and nature of the phenomenon

The Government of India has an elaborate mechanism to collect educational statistics, with data relating to numerical and financial information on schools, examination results and the participation of specified groups. Many national and state bodies are also involved in collecting and analysing data at different levels. Delays, reliability and usability of the data are the main limitations observed. In 2003, the District Information System for Education (DISE) was introduced as the national EMIS and has now emerged as a stable and comprehensive data source. It is limited in that it does not have data on unrecognised schools, though it does have information on recognised schools (which offers the trends unfolding across the country). Despite limitations, DISE remains the one comprehensive data source. Some of the outcomes of analysing DISE data and other available research are below:

- Around 16.86 per cent (or 189,512) schools are privately managed, of which 33.46 per cent are aided schools. The proportion of children attending unrecognised schools varies from around 5–40 per cent in different states.

- Over the past few years, private schools have grown consistently both in number and in the proportion of the education sector that they represent.

- Though private schools have better infrastructure on paper, in reality they offer very poor conditions. Government schools are also closing the infrastructure gap.

- Government primary schools had an average of 2.63 teachers per school compared to 4.74 in private schools. The latter are, however, paid a fraction of the salary that a government teacher gets.

- Private schools have an enrolment somewhat higher than their share of schools, implying that they are 'eating into' government school clientele.

- There is a preponderance of disadvantaged groups (girls, scheduled castes and scheduled tribes) in government schools.

- A study of unrecognised schools in Punjab reveals that the share of unrecognised enrolment to total enrolment in recognised and unrecognised schools is as high as 26 per cent, and that the existing GER of 51.73 per cent would alter to 66.27 per cent were the enrolment into unrecognised schools taken into account. This clearly casts doubt on any planning exercise that only uses data on the registered schools as its basis.

Collecting data on unrecognised schools, finding ways of recording dual enrolment, collecting information on socio-economic background students and fees charged, and involving private schools as partners in universalisation emerge as requirements.

The demand for low-fee private education

Such research as is available confirms that the number of private schools has grown dramatically over the last decade. Apart from a compound annual growth rate of 9.5 per cent in enrolment in (primary) private schools between 1986 and 1993, the number of private-unaided primary schools increased six-fold and private-recognised schools three-fold between 1970 and 2002. Another study notes that 28 per cent of the rural population had access to fee-charging private primary schools in the same village, of which 50 per cent had been recently established and which had 40 per cent of the private school enrolment.

It is also apparent that the poor are increasingly accessing these schools. Parent perceptions of better quality and greater accountability of such schools obviously inform this decision. Scholarships for the poor in private schools in some states and the lure of an 'English Medium' education also have an impact. Though some researchers have welcomed this development, others have lamented that the mushrooming of these 'teaching shops' reflects the state's willingness to allow a 'private solution to a public deficiency.'

Case studies

Field visits were undertaken to a rural and a peri-urban location in India's most populous state, Uttar Pradesh, which ranks low on the Educational Development Index. All the rural schools visited were located close to, and had a high degree of migration from, government schools. They had fees ranging from 30–50 Indian rupees (Rs)[1] and functioned for considerably more days than did government schools. They had minimal, crude and cramped accommodation with hardly any facilities. A few educational 'props' such as learning material and even a computer were randomly on display, but not seem to be in use. These schools focus on *appearing* to be good schools in the eyes of consumers (often illiterate parents), who rely on these trappings to assess the quality of a school against its competitors.

Teacher-pupil ratios in the schools ranged from 1:40 to 1:50, with children coming from the most marginalised sections, from families with low socio-economic status. Most teachers had secondary education, but no other professional qualifications. Salaries in Uttar Pradesh were well below the minimum wage for unskilled labour and ranged from Rs.500–800 per month. Teachers looked upon this as a means to gain experience as they prepared for other jobs and teacher turnover is high; however, this does not trouble the schools since more teachers continue to be cheaply available.

Children are required to buy textbooks (unlike in government schools) and teaching is centred around lecturing or 'explaining' the lesson, with little effort to ensure that children have understood. Homework is heavy (though children do not have help at home). High teacher turnover prevents any continuity and teachers employ corporal punishment regularly to ensure compliance.

Parents of only a half to two-thirds of the children are able to pay even the low fees, and schools try to obtain government scholarships; these are released for the whole year, though after many delays and much commission. This compensates the schools somewhat. During vacations, teachers are not paid although fees are still being collected. Managers may make as little as Rs.2,000 a month. Often schools are opened by those from a 'higher' caste or social position, whose 'dignity' does not allow them to take up wage labour or petty shop keeping. This preserves their social standing. Also, as schools construct rooms one-at-a-time (when money comes in), they may eventually become 'owners of a large building', which serves as an incentive.

In urban areas, no child was found being provided with free education, and fee collection was regular. Extras such as uniforms (which schools were able to insist upon), transport and other charges added to the burden of parents. Interviews with parents brought out that a fee-paying school is considered to be worth it only when the child is ready, and also when he/she seems to be learning. One parent felt that, 'The quality of teaching or how well teachers teach depends on whose child it is. Teachers pay attention to those who are better off or whose father has some power .... When it comes to our children, they don't bother....'

Supply and quality issues

The quality of private school education is difficult to assess, with achievement tests being used as a proxy for quality of education. This is also limited to smaller samples, since there are no comparable nation- or state-wide tests. A study in one part of Delhi found children scoring 72–246 per cent higher than those in government schools. Another study in Lucknow, which took measures to control for social and personal factors, found that the performance of private school students was (statistically) significantly higher.

Given the miniscule coverage of such studies, many issues need to be researched further. Do private schools provide a greater 'value addition'? How do 'good' government schools compare with 'good' low-fee private schools? What would achievement results show if the tests/examinations went beyond mechanistic aspects of learning? And what is the quality of these schools per se?

In terms of school efficiency, research shows that despite higher unit costs, government schools had lower outputs, greater wastage and stagnation, and made much poorer use of resources compared to private schools.

It cannot be the poor quality of government schools alone that allows private schools to spring up, however. Competitive resourcefulness also plays a role. As the village saying goes, 'new private schools open once the crop is cut and there is money to invest.' A network of financial relationships and opening a 'coaching centre' near a government school are initial steps, along with the lure of scholarships. In many states, however, private schools prefer to remain unrecognised, since they can then get away with ignoring government conditions and paying teachers one-fifth the government salary.

With around half the children unable to pay fees regularly, the school tends to function at a subsistence level. Various researchers have called the monthly salaries of private school teachers inhuman as they range from Rs.600–2,000 across India. Despite this, the absence rate of private teachers is similar to or lower than that of government teachers.

Many researchers have also lamented the extremely poor quality of the private schools. At present the only effort to improve the quality of low fee schools is the EQUIP (Educational Quality Improvement Programme) of Catholic Relief Services (CRS) in UP. Between 2002 and 2007, EQUIP has been implemented in around 100 schools. It organises schools in clusters and enables indicator-based and phased improvement over a long period. A clear improvement in enrolment, as well as quality parameters, including learning levels, is visible. More important, there are several instances of increased community support to these schools.

Impact on the system

There are at least five areas where the impact of the private schools may be felt on the government school system:

1. Declining enrolment in government schools. In around a quarter of the districts across the country, enrolment in government schools is actually declining (without an increase in the number of out-of-school children).

2. Subsidies to the private sector and duplication eat into government resources. Both explicit subsidies (such as direct transfers to schools) and implicit subsidies (such as land at concessional rates) add up to 'massive' levels. Dual enrolment, too, leads to duplication of resources, and needs to be researched further.

3. Planning for universalisation is rendered incomplete, because indicators such as GER and NER do not take into account children enrolled in unrecognised schools.

4. Inequity is increased as the system's performance decreases: as more powerful families withdraw from the public system, its accountability decreases. Those remaining are the more vulnerable groups, who are seen as receiving a 'favour' rather than a public service that is their right. They are blamed for not providing sufficient inputs to their children. As one of the parents interviewed said, 'How well teachers teach depends on whose child it is...'

5. Finally, the notion of education itself is diluted: this is because private schools cater to a 'pop' notion of what a good school should be, which tends to be more about appearance than reality. Unfortunately, the government is trying to imitate private schools by adopting some of their questionable practices, including the teaching of English from the first year of schooling.

Options ahead

Given that regulation of private schools focuses on inputs rather than processes or outcomes, it is difficult to envisage an improvement resulting from a tightening of such regulation. Discussion on options ahead tends to revolve around the following (limited) possibilities:

1. Bringing about a common school system – which tends to defy reality given the extent to which the private schools have grown.

2. Compelling private schools to offer free places to the poor – which requires schools to be discrimination-free and classless, which society itself is not.

3. Ensuring that the private system is properly regulated – which has not generated results over the last few decades.

4. Letting the market determine or facilitating an 'aided choice' (such as vouchers). However, the market tends to favour the 'pop' (and questionable) notion of education. Offering a completely subsidised social good, education establishments of the government are not open to the kind of 'pressure' that competition might lead to. Given its huge scale, the government system is not one that can be wished away.

5. Improving the government system – which, as the poor quality being attained by the government's EFA programme reveals, is not so easy.

6. Improving the private sector – which is also difficult, because as long as the schools can make a profit they have no incentive to improve.

In this context, the recently passed Right to Education Bill asserts every child's right by ensuring a school in every child's neighbourhood and the provision of free education to all children in government schools. However, it does not seek to alter the present provision through private, aided and unaided schools. It does make certification mandatory, which brings about dangers of corruption and undue interference in management. The Bill is also mired in debates and political pressures and at the time of writing had not been operationalised.

In a situation such as this, it is sustained and low-key action that is more likely to work. Three possibilities are indicated:

1. Collecting data from unrecognised schools, building their confidence in order to enable this;

2. Supporting the improvement of quality in private schools and their emergence as partners in universalising education; and

3. Developing process and outcome parameters for **all** schools to attain and educating parents to generate public insistence on quality. Building institutional capacity to attain these standards would be critical, as would involving stakeholders

such as parents and community representatives in monitoring the quality of the system.

Such democratic, decentralising steps might lead the multiple stakeholders to ask appropriate questions and enable them to work towards answers most suited to their contexts.

School types in India and low-cost private education

Private schools

As commercial institutions that derive profit from providing education to a non-elite clientele, private schools have a history of more than two decades in India. Up until the early 1970s, both government and private schools charged the same fee levels. Then in the early 1970s, key central legislations led to fees being abolished in government schools and the extension of public funding to private schools through grant-in-aid, which resulted in such schools also abolishing fees. Such private schools that received government funding came to be known as 'private-aided' or just 'aided' schools. They are managed by private bodies, but it is the government that selects and appoints the teachers, and regulations that apply to government schools are also in force. Thus these schools are virtually an extension of the government school system.

Contrasted to these, there are private-*unaided* (or just 'private') schools that generate their revenues through fees and are managed entirely by private bodies without any government intervention. Private schools also fall into two categories: recognised and unrecognised. Recognised private schools are those that comply to a number of conditions laid down by government (such as having their own – rather than a rented – building; having trained teachers who are paid salaries according to pre-scribed norms; not being located within five kilometres of a government school; and several other requirements). Recognised schools are also required to provide infor-mation to the government from time to time. In practice of course, recognition is often obtained by means other than complying with the prescribed conditions. It is commonly known that hardly any private schools that get recognition fulfil all the conditions of recognition.

Schools seek recognition because this entitles them to issue the transfer certificates needed by students to take admission into upper primary and higher classes, as well as to be eligible to receive some government provisions, including scholarships for certain categories of students. The biggest benefit of recognition, though, is that it confers a degree of legitimacy and leads to a more positive perception in the eyes of the consumers, and hence increases the likelihood of higher enrolment, leading to higher revenues.

Study of Unrecognised Schools in Punjab by Arun Mehta

'So far as recognised schools are concerned, examinations are conducted either by the school itself or by the local School Board. No information, however, is available in this regard so far as examination results reported by unrecognised schools are concerned. However, it is a common practice that children continue to enrol in unrecognised schools till terminal grade but they appear in examination conducted by a recognised school/board. Examination, if conducted by unrecognised schools, is not recognised elsewhere. This raises the issue of dual enrolment. Children in a terminal grade enrolled in an unrecognised school are also enrolled in a recognised school, without which they cannot appear in examination conducted by a recognised school or board. They attend unrecognised schools all through the year, appear in examinations conducted by recognised schools and if passed, transit to recognised schools for further studies. This is a general perception that needs to be further probed and examined. This also raises a vital question: why do parents prefer unrecognised to recognised schools? They are ready to pay tuition and other fees, provided that quality education is ensured, or it may be because of English as the medium of instruction.'

Source: Mehta, 2005.

Schools accessed by the poor for their low fees belong to both the recognised and the unrecognised sector. However, it is apparent that the informal, unrecognised sector is the one that has witnessed the greatest growth and has emerged as a major avenue for education among the poorer sections. In keeping with this, the study focuses upon the informal private sector (the unrecognised private schools serving the poorest sections of India's population) to the fullest extent possible.

Poor-oriented, profit-based private schools

Apart from being distinct from aided and recognised schools, unrecognised private schools are also different from other categories of schools that the poor might send their children to. One major category of such schools is those set up by philanthropic organisations (usually trusts) and NGOs (both charitable and 'development' oriented). Such schools typically address the needs of identified groups of poorest or most disadvantaged children, such as those in slums or tribal areas, or children with disabilities. Sometimes schools set up by trusts favour specific communities (e.g. Gujarati children) or language/ethnic groups (such as Sanskrit schools or schools with a south Indian language as a medium of instruction being established in north India, where these languages are not spoken).

A number of NGO-run schools are intended to be 'innovative' and *adapt* the existing curriculum, pedagogies and materials or develop their own. However, the main sources of funding for these organisations remain donors – members of the public, philanthropists, donor agencies and even governments. Commitment to the needs of the poor and a strong ideological orientation (especially in the NGO schools) also tends to be visible. Of late, some corporate bodies have also stepped in to set up hundreds of schools for the poor, as part of their corporate social responsibility. Again, the costs of such schools are underwritten by these mammoth corporate bodies, which have emerged as part of India's recent 'growth story'.

A second category of schools for the poor are those of religious/faith-based organisations. Among these, both 'traditional' (or religion-oriented) and 'modern' (or relatively secular) forms may be observed. Hindu organisations run '*gurukuls*', which offer education with an emphasis on scriptural knowledge; they also run 'Sanskrit schools', which focus on the classical language and knowledge. *Madrasas* are commonly available to poor Muslim communities across the country (there being Boards of Madrasa Education in many states). They are often the only resort for poor Muslim children, especially girls who may be allowed to attend the *madrasa* rather than the local government school.

Religious organisations also run 'modern' or secular schools that follow the state curricula, incorporate many practices of high-end private schools and charge a moderate fee. These schools are heavily subsidised by their parent bodies, are informed by the zeal and fervour of those who run them and have an openly religious orientation along with offering secular education. (However, both Christian and Hindu organisations also run many elite schools that charge high fees.)

From all such schools, therefore, the low-fee private school stands apart. It is distinguished by relying solely on the fees collected as a source of survival, and those who start such schools may have no background in education or any particular concern with it, since this is mainly a business opportunity. Such schools are compelled to attract and retain children through a range of means (which might sometimes include the actual education that takes place in them). Their functioning is governed by market mechanisms rather than any specific ideological, intellectual, religious or spiritual disposition or slant. Economic efficiency overrides all other considerations, and aggressive positioning among potential clients is what helps them compete with a large number of other inexpensive schools in the vicinity with very similar features. That the number of such schools has grown dramatically over the last two decades in a country where a widespread government education system offers free education (and other incentives) is as much due to their strenuous entrepreneurial efforts as the increasingly self-evident dysfunctional nature of the government school system in India.

The emergence of the inexpensive schools

Interestingly, in some ways the government system has actually contributed to the growth of low-fee private schools.

Starting from the 1990s, the Government of India launched large-scale primary and elementary education programmes that laid tremendous emphasis on enrolment of children (in fact, these efforts are still under way). Demand was generated through community awareness efforts throughout the country, using village contact programmes, the electronic media, partnering thousands of NGOs, establishing village education committees (or other groups such as mother-teacher associations) and of course opening a large number of schools (only with provision actually being there could many communities consider education for their children). Apart from community mobilisation, a range of incentives was also made available as entitlements, especially to the poorest sections of society – such as midday meals, free textbooks, uniforms and the like. All this activity led to a dramatic growth in the school-going population, while also raising parental awareness and aspirations. Thus from 1999–2005, the number of primary schools in India grew from 642,000 to 767,520, with enrolment (in primary schools) increasing from 113.61 million to 131.69 million. In the same years, the GER moved from 94.9 to 108.6 for the primary level.

As government schools opened rapidly across the country and people began sending their children to them, parental dissatisfaction also began to be evident. The poor quality of the government schools was reflected in the frequently absent or 'present-but-not-teaching' teacher, low levels of learning attained by children ('my child can't even write his name after three years in school'), and the highly visible corruption that the community began to see in its dealings with the school (whether with the midday meal or other entitlements, or vis-à-vis the village education committees).

It must be said that not all government schools/efforts were of such poor quality; indeed in many states innovative measures led to a vibrant educational scenario, with one project even leading a reduction in private school enrolment in Kerala. However, *public perceptions of the poor quality of government schools* were also an extension of existing notions about government provision – for example, government health services have always been considered poorer than private ones, with people preferring to pay for the chance to regain their health rather than continue to be *'ill for free'!*

Local entrepreneurs stoked this dissatisfaction and began to offer a competing, low-cost product/service. As economic growth led to more people emerging above the poverty line and others moving into higher income brackets, the number of those who could now consider paying (a low fee) for education also began to increase. All this became possible since it was actually the government programmes that generated the demand for education.

This is also reflected in large-scale dual enrolment, whereby children draw entitlements from the government school while actually studying in a private school. (This data is unfortunately very difficult to obtain, though it is widely reported across the country). One outcome of dual enrolment is of course duplication and wastage of effort and resources (e.g. government expenditure on teachers is being made irrespective of whether they have sufficient students or whether those students are learning – indeed a recent government publication points out that the average primary student takes *9.08 years compared to the ideal of 5 years to graduate* (Mehta, 2007 [DISE,[2] Analytical Report 2005–06]). Equally critical is that the situation has led to a distortion in the notion of education among a large section of the poor, where it is the trappings and appearance of a school, rather than the actual outcomes in the form of desired learning, that are taken to be education. Private schools have successfully created this 'image-oriented' notion, and have reaped its benefit (this is elaborated upon in later sections).

What is a low-fee school?

What would be called an inexpensive school or a low-fee school? Different researchers have used criteria such as comparison to a day's wage or similar reference points (Muralidharan & Kremer, 2006). The variation in such schools, however, is so great that such reference points lack the elasticity to cover this. Two ways of looking at these schools are as follows:

- *Low-fee private schools are typically those used by the poorest fee-paying population in any area.* Those poorer than these groups will be able to send their children only to government schools, or not educate them at all. There is also a degree of overlap in the sense that these groups definitely need and desire the entitlements available in the government system (such as the midday meal or uniforms), leading to dual enrolments. Perhaps the best term for the poorest fee-paying groups is the 'emerging poor'. Often the economic conditions and the commitment to education of these groups is of a borderline nature, implying that children may move out of schools, shift to government schools or even sit at home until another push takes place.

- 'Low-fee' may be seen as a range where the lower-middle- to lower-income groups (almost up to those bordering the poverty line) send their children. In the schools that were visited, the monthly fees (along with other school related expenses) tended to be around 2(+) days' earnings for a typical daily wage worker of the area.

Tracking the scale and nature of the phenomenon

Data availability and quality

While the Government of India (GoI) has an elaborate mechanism to collect educational statistics and release them on an annual basis, its focus has tended to be mainly on data related to government schools. The data collected is related to numerical and financial information on schools, examination results and participation of specified groups such as scheduled castes and scheduled tribes. At the state level, Directorates of Education have specialised planning and statistics cells responsible for collecting, processing and disseminating data. These are supported by a skeleton staff in the office of the district education officer. This data is collated by the Ministry of Human Resource Development at the national level and published on an annual basis, though the time lags involved reduce its usefulness. As the Statistical Commission appointed by the Government of India in 2000 noted, 'There are major deficiencies of data,... [which] include: poor quality of data collected by the statistical system, inordinate delays, lack of effective checks, incomplete coverage, inconsistent data, poor implementation of provisions of Acts, low priority and general apathy to statistical activities, inadequate infrastructure and staff for statistical work, and lack of computerisation and its use in data compilation, processing and dissemination of data produced by different agencies.'

In 2003, the District Information System for Education (DISE, described later) was introduced as the national EMIS and the country is in a transition stage where the GoI's annual statistics have not yet been abandoned, even though DISE is in place. Apart from this, many national and state bodies are also involved in collecting and analysing data at different levels. The more readily accessible ones are mentioned below:

- All India Education Surveys of the National Council for Educational Research and Training (NCERT), conducted every five years (though running behind time for the last three surveys), provides information on accessibility and availability of various types of facilities in schools. This survey often tends to be an unwieldy exercise, since it is implemented with the support of state education departments and lacks a permanent structure.

- The Census of India is conducted once a decade and provides comprehensive household-level data at various degrees of aggregation/disaggregation. It includes information on school attendance among the school-age population (at least on a sample basis).

- National Sample Surveys (NSS) conducted by the National Sample Survey Organisation collect information from selected households on a sample basis, with each round focusing on specific areas of social and economic activity. The NSS data classifies respondents' educational and other characteristics by social and economic status (e.g. distribution of households by their educational attainment cross-classified by income fractile group). Unfortunately, this data is not always available in full form to researchers, and the validity of NSS data has not yet been established through independent research.

- Surveys conducted by different national bodies from time to time. Organisations such as NCERT have conducted surveys of learning achievement across the country. Similarly, the All India Educational Administration Surveys are conducted by the National University of Educational Planning and Administration (NUEPA). A major NGO, Pratham, has also conducted a 'citizen's survey' called the Annual Status of Education Report (ASER), involving a large number of NGOs across the country.

- State-level educational statistics. These are considerably more detailed than those available at the national level, though they vary from state to state. Only Punjab and Orissa (and to some extent Andhra Pradesh) have included unrecognised private schools in their data collection exercises (and have found that they account for at least one-fourth the children attending school). Again, inadequate and ill-equipped staffing affects the timeliness and reliability of the data.

Each of the sources mentioned above has major limitations of its own, apart from the fact that private schools (even the aided ones) are not covered. While the data available has been examined (and used in places), this study relies mainly on the DISE, which is described below.

District Information System for Education (DISE)

It was in the mid-1990s that a computer-based EMIS was initiated in India with the launch of the large-scale District Primary Education Programme, which eventually covered half the country. This EMIS, renamed DISE by 2000, focused on creating a database on all key variables related to access, participation, teachers, facilities and infrastructure. In 2003, DISE was extended to the entire country as the official data reporting system for elementary education (DISE, 2006). By 2007, it provided a fairly stable and comprehensive time series data, which is regularly made available on an annual basis.

DISE data is collected from schools through sub-district structures (cluster resource centres and block resource centres), with data capture formats, definitions and concepts being uniform across states. Data is entered and compiled in DISE software at the district level from where it is aggregated at state and national levels. Over the last decade, DISE coverage, at least for the government educational system, has been near universal, with details of 1.04 million schools and 4.17 million teachers being available on a number of variables. Information is increasingly available over the Internet, moving towards enabling planners and decision-makers at various levels to access it. The nodal body, the National University of Educational Planning and Administration (NUEPA), also publishes this information and its analyses for wider dissemination, while raw data is available to researchers. In the last three years, DISE has also begun to include information on private schools (though the focus is mainly on aided private schools).

Limitations from the study's point of view

Some of the limitations of DISE arise due to its scale and varying skill levels of the EMIS staff, along with frequent changes of personnel in some states. Outsourcing of data entry also affects accuracy of information. A critical issue is that in some respects the coverage is not complete – with the major omission being that of private-unaided schools (and other categories, such as open schools or other kinds of informal provision being made available). Nor have many of the (recognised) private schools chosen to respond to DISE efforts (and there is no legislation mandating provision of such information). Even among private schools' data, since neither school fees is included nor the socio-economic background of the students, it is not possible to

Lack of Data

Many researchers have been frustrated by lack of data. Here, for instance, is Kingdon (2005):

'Analysis of education in India in general and of private and public schools in particular is hampered by the lack of availability of data. Despite recent improvements in the educational database in India, there is a serious paucity of reliable educational data in India. Firstly, the official data collection exercise on schools (both annually and in the periodic 'All India Education Surveys') collects information only on the so-called 'recognised' schools. Thus, large numbers of private schools are not included in the official data since they are 'unrecognised'. Secondly, coverage of even the recognised schools is incomplete. For instance, coverage of various types of special schools is patchy across different states, such as Central Schools, Army Schools, Education Guarantee Schools, schools registered with national examination boards, etc. Thirdly, enrolment figures in school-returns data are unreliable because failing/unpopular publicly-funded schools exaggerate their student numbers in order to justify their existence. Fourthly, no national-, state- or district-level data are collected on student learning achievement in primary and junior education in private and public schools; while exam boards do have achievement data for **secondary** school level, these are not publicly available to researchers and in any case, they are not linked to student, teacher and school characteristics.

---

extract information on whether the needs of the poor and the marginalised are being served, and to what extent.

In some state reports, consistency of data is also an issue; specific information (e.g. school-age population or age and grade of children) may also be missing. The DISE national team has used projected values from other sources to overcome these lacunae. Since entitlements such as midday meals and even the posting of teachers are linked to enrolment figures, it is possible that school personnel are sometimes wary of revealing changes that might be occurring due to the proliferation of low-fee private schools. During field visits, it is certainly apparent that the system is unable to take into account children who are enrolled in the government school (for entitlements) and actually attend the low-fee private school (for education). At times, the district and state authorities too wish to project a certain image of the state and may manipulate figures such as the percentage of children enrolled in government schools.

Despite these limitations, DISE remains the one major source of information about the school system, and the indicators it captures do provide sufficient basis to infer the evolving status of the primary and elementary education system in India. Indeed, the quality of information available in DISE is so much more recent, comprehensive and reliable than all other sources, this study uses DISE data as a major source in the sections that follow.

Data on private schools from DISE 2005–06

In the figures given below, the reference to private schools is limited to *recognised* private schools, and the ones that *chose* to share information with DISE. In that sense, although these figures provide a broad picture of the spread and nature of private schools, they are by no means an accurate representation of the situation on the ground. At the same time, a fair proportion of these recognised private schools are low-fee ones where the poor send their children. Also, as indicated earlier, children in unrecognised schools might be enrolled in recognised schools in terminal grades for purposes of obtaining valid certification, in which case data from the recognised schools might incorporate some children of unrecognised schools as well. For these reasons, and because it is the only comprehensive data source that is available, DISE is being used to identify (at least indirectly) the scale and nature of the phenomenon. Later, some state-specific available data is presented.

The bulleted points below quote the relevant data from DISE analysis.

Spread of schools

- Of the total 1,124,033 schools in India (i.e. those captured in DISE), around 83.14 per cent (or 934,521) are government-run schools, with around 16.86 per cent (or 189,512) being privately managed (i.e. they include both the aided and the unaided schools).

- Within privately managed schools, 33.46 per cent (or 63,411) are private aided schools, with the remaining 66.54 per cent (or 126,100) being private unaided schools.

The number of unrecognised private schools is not available on a national basis. However, a study conducted by Aggarwal (2000) in four districts revealed around 25 per cent children attending such schools and he estimated that across the country the figures would vary from 5–40 per cent.

- The state-wide distribution of schools run by private-aided management is as high as 56.19 per cent in Kerala.

It is not as if private schools are concentrated in areas considered to have poor quality education/system. In the case of Kerala, which is fairly high up in the Educational Development Index (an official ranking of states on various parameters), the number and percentage of private schools is the highest. Similarly, other highly-ranked states such as Karnataka also report a high percentage of private-aided schools.

The percentage of private schools is growing

- Government schools can be run by a variety of different government departments in India. The proportion of government schools run by the Department of Education consistently declined from 61.06 per cent in 2002–03 to 57.64 per cent in 2005–06.

- On an average, 63.44 per cent of the total primary schools are being run by the Department of Education itself compared to 68.46 per cent of the total independent upper primary schools being run by it.

- The percentage of schools being run by the Tribal/Social Welfare Department is only 4.51 per cent of the total schools.

- The share of schools under local authority management has declined, from 20.89 per cent in 2003-04 to 19.85 per cent of schools in 2005-06.

- Over a period of time, schools run under private-aided as well as private-unaided management have increased.

- Between 2004-05 and 2005-06, the number of private schools that reported data under DISE operations increased by 31,253 schools, which was 20.51 per cent of the private schools during the previous year.

The number of private schools being reported in DISE has been increasing over the last three years – this points not only to the increased coverage of DISE, but also to the increase in the numbers of private schools.

Infrastructure

- Irrespective of the school type, schools imparting elementary education across 604 districts in 2005-06 had an average of 3.8 classrooms.

- All schools together have an average of 39 students per classroom (rural 40 and urban 35 students per class). Government schools have a student classroom ratio of 40:1 against 29:1 in the case of schools managed by private management.

- Of the total of schools that do not have buildings, as many as 96.94 per cent of such schools are being run by government management.

'Don't Ask, Don't Tell'

The surprise is not in the absolute number of private schools, but their proliferation rate. Nearly 50 per cent of the rural private schools accounted for in the (2006) study conducted by Harvard economists Michael Kremer and Karthik Muralidharan were established after 2000, and nearly 40 per cent of private school enrolment is in these new schools Regulatory gaps and dissatisfaction with government schools are the key factors driving the demand for private schooling. There is already evidence of such a surge in Punjab, Haryana, Uttar Pradesh, Andhra Pradesh, West Bengal, Karnataka, Meghalaya and Delhi. In seven districts of Punjab, 86 per cent of the private schools are unrecognised. A majority of these private-unrecognised schools are operating outside the scope of policy-makers' radars. It is a 'don't ask, don't tell' situation. Officials think of it as a fringe phenomenon. Consequently, these schools do not make it into any of the education statistics compiled by education departments.

Source: Mandava, N. p.23 (2007)

It might appear that the infrastructure figures favour private schools. What is not captured in the figures is the actual space available – most private schools are little more than an extension of the owner's house and have small, hovel-like rooms with little light and ventilation. Children sit crowded in and there is no space for the teacher to move. Such sub-human conditions are not 'noticed' by children and their parents – school managers tend to think that they come from such poor conditions themselves that this is not so bad for them! Similar conditions have been reported by other researchers as well, especially De, Noronha & Samson (2002).

Basic facilities

- Only 83.07 per cent schools (including all categories) had drinking water available in 2005–06 compared to 80.60 per cent in the previous year.

- As compared to 81 per cent schools under government management, more than 93 per cent schools under private management had drinking water facilities.

- As compared to 70.57 per cent of private schools with common toilets, in the case of government management this figure is as low as 48.95 per cent.

The government system is rapidly catching up in terms of infrastructure and facilities, with the countrywide implementation of the *Sarva Shiksha Abhiyan* (as the country's EFA effort is known). With the formation of Village Education Committees and School Management Committees drawn from the parents and the community, money for school repairs, construction and maintenance is being routed through these groups. Thus, in the last few years government school infrastructure has begun to match or exceed that available in low-fee private schools. However, poor maintenance of the new infrastructure, due to lack of ownership and motivation on part of teachers, at times tends to negate the gains made.

- It is interesting to note that the percentage of primary schools with a ramp is higher (16.35 per cent) for schools under government management than those under private management (9.43 per cent).

This is mainly due to the recent emphasis on inclusion of children with disabilities in government schools, and the provision of grants for construction.

- More schools in urban areas (58.07 per cent) arranged medical check-ups for the students than schools in rural areas (52.80 per cent).

- The percentage of privately-managed schools (57.07 per cent) that arranged medical check-ups was slightly higher than government managed schools (52.71 per cent).

Staffing

- Schools managed by government have a much higher percentage of single-teacher schools (14.13 per cent) compared to privately-managed schools (2.87 per cent).

- A little more than half of the total schools are yet to be provided with regular headmasters. Fewer schools in rural areas (46.04 per cent) have headmasters than schools in urban areas (52.65 per cent).

Teacher-related indicators

- More teachers are available in urban areas and in private schools. The availability of teachers in rural areas is 3.76 teachers per school, while in urban areas it is 7.40 teachers per school. In schools managed by government there are 3.62 teachers per school, while in those managed privately there are 7.10 teachers per school.
- The average number of teachers in government schools is about half of the average number in privately-managed schools.
- All primary schools managed by government had an average of 2.63 teachers per school compared to 4.74 teachers in privately-managed schools.
- The percentage of women teachers in government schools has been low at 35.77 per cent; this compares to 47.72 per cent in the case of private schools.

Teacher-related indicators is clearly one area where private schools are better off. A vast majority of government schoolteachers handle multi-grade situations compared to those in private schools (exact figures are not available, but this may be inferred; during field visits too, no private schoolteacher was found teaching more than one grade at a time, whereas this was commonly seen in government schools). Also, it is not only the greater number of teachers per school, but their actual presence (with a higher teaching time) that makes a difference. Private schools achieve these numbers by paying teachers far less than the government schoolteacher, and appointing them on a short-term basis.

Teacher-pupil ratio

- Irrespective of school types, an improvement in teacher-pupil ratio has been observed during the period 2002–03 to 2005–06.
- All schools together show that Bihar, with 65 students per teacher, had the highest ratio and Sikkim, with 15, the lowest ratio. Bihar also has a high teacher-pupil ratio of 47 even amongst schools with private management.

Enrolment-based indicators

- The average government enrolment is as high as 90.75 per cent (of children from the school's catchment area). This compares to only 59.10 per cent for private management schools.
- 83.14 per cent of schools in India are managed by government and 16.86 per cent are managed privately.

Teacher Characteristics

A key question that follows the discussion on teacher pay in private schools is that of understanding who the private schoolteachers are, and the reasons for their being willing to work at such low salaries. Field visits suggest that the availability of these inexpensive teachers in villages is being driven by local educated youth who are typically unable to find jobs, unwilling (and seldom needed) to work in agriculture, and who are not looking at teaching as a long-term career. Teaching suits these youth well because the short working day of 4–6 hours allows them the time for further study via correspondence (distance-education) courses or in colleges that open at suitable times. The short working days also allow them to look for other, longer-term jobs on the side, and finally teaching provides them with both income and respectability while they look for other, long-term options.

.... The private schoolteachers are on average more than 10 years younger than their counterparts in the public sector, and are twice as likely to be from the village where the school is located. They are more likely to have a college degree, but also much less likely to have a professional teaching certificate. This suggests that even though they are more educated, they are not looking at teaching as a long-term career option.

This probably helps to explain why teacher absence is not even lower in private schools, given the high likelihood of action being taken for repeated absence. Since private schoolteachers are being paid a much lower wage and are often looking out for other, long-term options, there is little 'efficiency wage' cost of being fired. Thus, if pursuing other opportunities requires a certain level of absence (and an accompanying probability of action being taken) this is a trade off that the private schoolteachers are probably willing to make. However, in spite of the low wages, we see that private schools have lower teacher absence and higher teaching activity than the public schools – especially in the same village.

Source: Muralidharan & Kremer (2006) pp. 14–15.

- However, enrolment in privately-managed schools is somewhat higher than their share of schools. All government schools together had 72.61 per cent of the total elementary enrolment (primary and upper primary).

- About 90 per cent of primary schools in 2005–06 were under government management, with an enrolment of only 82.78 per cent.

The above data clearly shows that private schools are 'eating into' the clientele of government schools. If one takes into account dual enrolment, the overlap is likely to be much higher, implying that the number of children attending government schools is much less.

There is also some information that runs counter to what is reported in DISE. A countrywide sample survey of households conducted during July-October 2005 (SRI-IMRB, 2005) collected data from a sample of 87,874 households and found the following:

Among those who are reported to be attending school in the age group 6–13, an overwhelming 84.2 per cent are in government schools, 13.3 per cent in private-recognised schools, 1.8 per cent in private-unrecognised schools and 0.7 per cent in AIE (alternative and innovative education) centres, *Madrasas*, etc.

These figures do not fully account for the sheer number of private schools and it is likely that households reported government enrolment (for fear of losing out on entitlements) where a child was actually attending a private school.

Education for the disadvantaged

- The percentage of girls' enrolment in government-managed schools was found to be higher than in privately-managed schools.

- Notably, at all levels, government has been the main provider and caterer of the educational needs of both scheduled caste (SC) and scheduled tribe (ST) children. The percentage of SC enrolment in primary classes is as high as 84.39; schools under private managements had only 15.61 per cent of the total SC primary enrolment, and only 11.40 per cent of such enrolment in upper primary.

- Both SC and ST enrolment together had a share of 80.34 and 85.80 per cent respectively in primary and upper primary levels of education in schools under government management.

This information reinforces the commonly held view that people prefer to educate their daughters in government schools and pay fees for their sons' education. It also indicates that government school is clearly the main recourse for the more disadvantaged groups. Conversely, private schools are educating those who have more supportive conditions at home and in society. The struggles that parents undertake to educate their children are also a sign of parental will, which likely impacts the nature of the child's participation in school. Thus improved levels of learning attained by these children are not necessarily a function of the school alone (all things not being same). Research that argues in favour of private schools on the grounds of the learning achievement of children may not be taking into account that two very different kinds of student populations are being compared.

A study of unrecognised private schools in Punjab

In 2005, the state of Punjab expanded its DISE to cover unrecognised schools. As a pilot, this was implemented in seven of the 17 districts of the state. An analysis of this data was completed by Mehta (2005) of NUEPA, and is extensively quoted below to highlight the kind of information that such data might throw up in many parts of the country. Unfortunately, the fee charged was not included as an indicator, nor was the socio-economic background of students, which makes it difficult to separate the information pertaining to the low-fee private school. The present data includes high-fee, unrecognised private schools (such schools opt to remain unrecognised since they do not wish to come under government purview in any manner and rely on their own reputation for success), which may tend to skew the analysis somewhat. [Comments in square brackets are the authors' own interpolations.]

From Mehta's Punjab study

The main objectives of the present study are to examine the pattern and number of unrecognised schools and enrolment in them.

The *school and teacher related indicators* reveal that unrecognised schools differ from recognised schools mainly in the following aspects:

- Unrecognised schools are less rural than the recognised schools;
- Unrecognised schools have slightly higher percentage of co-educational schools than the recognised schools. [This increases the consumer base];
- Unrecognised schools are generally more than one-teacher schools compared to recognised schools, which have relatively more single-teacher schools;
- Unrecognised schools have more favourable student-classroom and teacher-pupil ratios than the recognised schools;
- Unrecognised schools have a much greater percentage of female teachers than the recognised schools;
- Although the majority of the teachers in the unrecognised schools do not possess any professional teaching qualification, teachers in unrecognised schools are still better qualified than teachers in recognised schools;
- The percentage of English-medium unrecognised schools is much higher than the percentage of English-medium recognised schools; and
- Unrecognised schools do not have provision for in-service training of teachers, whereas more than half of the recognised school teachers had received in-service training during the previous year.

With regard to *facilities in unrecognised schools,* it is observed that:

- Unrecognised schools have more pre-primary sections attached to them than the recognised schools;
- School facilities are generally better in unrecognised schools than in the recognised ones; and
- The following aspects are more favourable in unrecognised schools compared to recognised schools: average number of instructional rooms, rooms in good condition, single-classroom schools, average number of teachers, computers in schools, common and girls' toilets, electricity connection, drinking water facilities etc.

Enrolment indicators reveal that unrecognised schools differ from recognised schools in the following aspects [authors' emphases]:

- A large number of children are enrolled in unrecognised schools, which is more than 37 per cent of total enrolment in recognised schools;

- Against every three students enrolled in recognised schools, more than one is enrolled in unrecognised schools;

- The share of unrecognised enrolment to total enrolment in recognised and unrecognised schools is as high as 26 per cent;

- The percentage of boys' enrolment in unrecognised schools is a bit higher than girls' enrolment;

- Compared to a GPI (Gender Parity Index) in elementary enrolment of 0.88 in recognised schools, the same in unrecognised schools is low at 0.68;

- For every 100 boys there are only 68 girls enrolled in unrecognised schools. [This is in keeping with the general perception of 'government schools for daughters, private schools for sons'];

- Percentage of enrolment in grade 1 in total primary enrolment is a bit higher for unrecognised schools than for recognised schools. [This indicates that parents often start children's education in such schools before shifting them to recognised schools as terminal grades approach];

- Average enrolment in unrecognised schools is higher than in recognised schools;

- Of the total SC enrolment, 9.25 per cent are enrolled in unrecognised and 90.75 per cent in recognised schools;

- More than 37 per cent of the total 947,000 out-of-school 6–14 year olds are enrolled in unrecognised schools. [This data reveals the extent to which the state government's universalisation effort may be functioning in the dark];

- Against a GER of 51.73 per cent, the corresponding GER based on both recognised and unrecognised enrolment is 66.27 per cent; and

- The percentage of children passing out terminal grade 5 and 8 with 60 per cent and above marks is higher in unrecognised schools than in recognised schools.

Improving data availability

The various limitations in available data have manifested themselves in the sections above and cast serious doubt on India's educational planning exercises. As Arun Mehta points out in the Punjab study quoted above:

'It is evident from enrolment statistics presented above that planning exercises based on enrolment data only from formal education system is not adequate. Unless enrolment in unrecognised sector is considered, the true picture of universal enrolment will never be known. The estimate of out-of-school children based on enrolment in recognised schools is a gross over-estimation of true number of out-of-school children.'

Given the apparent extent and rapidity of the phenomenon, much greater research is needed on the low-fee private school. Over the last three years, of the literally hundreds of research studies commissioned across India under the *Sarva Shiksha Abhiyan* (SSA, or the EFA programme), only four focused on private schools at all, and none specifically on unrecognised ones.

While the data availability situation has improved greatly over the years, especially with the introduction of DISE, a number of improvements still need to be built upon what has already been achieved. These improvements are suggested below:

- Clearly, data on unrecognised private schools needs to be collected, and fairly urgently. Although this is a challenging task, an administrative infrastructure already exists in the form of cluster and block resource centres, which would enable the government to extend the coverage of DISE to unrecognised schools (as was shown by the Punjab study, which needed just six months to obtain this information in seven districts). With the surge in IT-enabled and mobile services in India, these could easily be used to ensure rapid and accurate collection of data (e.g. the use of cheap, hand-held PDA-type devices using touch-screens in-stead of paper would reduce both cost and time, while increasing reliability, since a second round of data entry would not be involved).

- How can dual enrolment be recorded? This is a task in itself and needs to be addressed by a specialist group; what is apparent is that it is this particular factor that is compromising UPE data the most, thus affecting resource allocation and planning. (Such information would of course raise the policy issue of whether entitlements should still be issued to children who are paying fees to attend other schools, since the government is paying also for provision such as teachers, space and material that are not being utilised.)

- Capacity enhancement of personnel involved in data collection, analysis etc. at various levels is also needed in order to ensure the necessary coverage, reliability and consistency. At the same time, it is noted that there is insufficient use of available information to support planning and decision-making. Towards this, too, personnel at various levels need to be oriented in actually using the data they are responsible for.

- It is crucial to include the socio-economic background of students, as this would permit the kind of disaggregation needed (at present, it appears that political/administrative sensitivities have led to this not being permitted in DISE). This also makes it difficult to assess the degree of 'value addition' that the different categories of schools bring to children.

- Since information on fees and other requisites that families have to pay for is not collected (even from recognised schools), this makes it difficult to assess the cost to learners, or to take an informed view on the nature of provision (e.g. should 'school vouchers' be supported?) or the effectiveness of expenditure on education.

- All schools, government or private, recognised or unrecognised, tend to suspect government's reasons for data collection and fear penal action on some ground or another. At the same time, it is not mandatory for schools to share information. This naturally makes it difficult to obtain information, and there is a need to see schools as partners in the educational-planning process. Ways and means of reaching out to schools that would involve them in data collection (rather than their merely being subject to it) are needed, along with 'confidence-building' measures to convince schools that the purpose is not to ferret out flaws.

Some research questions

Among the key questions that need to be addressed, and might be better addressed if adequate information is made available as above, are:

- Why do schools choose to remain unrecognised?

- Why do parents choose unrecognised schools (sometimes over recognised ones), and why is such a strong rejection of the government school system visible even with provision of entitlements? This question has been addressed by different researchers and is much discussed; perhaps the answers are self-evident, but tracking children and the reasons for their shift still needs to be undertaken.

- Can the community or its representatives in the various school management committees be involved in understanding and using data regarding their children to bring about improvement?

- What factors are likely to enhance school performance and enable children to attain higher learning levels across both scholastic and non-scholastic objectives (the latter are not recorded anywhere at present)?

The demand for low-fee private education

The growth of private provision

Private schools have recorded a spurt in growth over the last decade and different researchers have recorded this phenomenon.

- In 1999, the Public Report on Basic Education (PROBE) pointed out that '36 per cent of the children in Uttar Pradesh, one of the poorest states in India, actually attend private schools', a number that might be difficult to verify now. Interestingly, this was regarded as a 'positive sign of the rising demand for education.'

- In his study 'Public and Private Partnership in Primary Education in India' Aggarwal (2000) observed that the enrolment (to primary classes) in private-aided schools rose at a compounded annual growth rate of 9.5 per cent between 1986 and 1993, while the corresponding figure for government/local body schools was 1.4 per cent. He estimated that the number of unrecognised schools was doubling every five years.

- While the number of private-unaided primary schools increased six-fold and private-recognised schools three-fold between 1970 and 2002, the number of government and local body schools fell by over 10 percentage points during the same period (Majumdar, 2003; Srivastava, 2007).

While the exact extent of low-fee private schools is difficult to ascertain, the scale may be estimated looking at data emerging from studies such as those by Muralidharan & Kremer (2006) and the Pratham ASER report (2005), of nationally representative samples of rural India. These showed the following:

- 28 per cent of the rural population had access to fee-charging private primary schools in the same village;

- 16.4 per cent of children aged 6–14 attended fee-charging private schools;

- nearly 50 per cent of these schools had been recently established (that is, 5 or fewer years before the survey); and

- nearly 40 per cent of private-school enrolment was in these recently-established schools.

In urban areas, the numbers and proportion of enrolment in private schools is widely believed to be significantly higher.

One school of researchers has welcomed this proliferation of private schools as a viable alternative being accessed by the poor. Prominent among them is Prof Tooley (2000), the title of one his studies itself capturing this view: 'The private sector serving the educational needs of the poor'. However, such 'mushrooming' does not find favour with everyone, with some taking an aggrieved tone at the state's willingness to allow a 'private solution to a public deficiency' (Majumdar, 2003), or at the encouragement of such 'teaching shops' by the government. The fact that the ideal of the common school system, long promised in various policies, has been relinquished and 'different types of schools for different sections' allowed to emerge (Srivastava, 2007) is also lamented. There is a feeling also that in pursuit of their own agendas, international donors (who were allowed entry to the education sector from the mid-1990s) have further stratified primary education (e.g. by supporting 'alternative education' models, or 'education guarantee' schools that are less equipped than formal primary schools in terms of staffing and infrastructure), compromising the quality of education that deprived children receive.

The inferiority of private schools also comes in for criticism. Srivastava (2007) points out that 'the situation has worsened further thanks to the unregulated mushrooming of English-medium nursery and primary schools, where classes are held all in one

room, on rooftops and under thatched roofs as feeders to the "teaching shops".'
Similarly, the SV Chittibabu Commission report (2003) on Tamil Nadu found nearly
23 per cent of the private schools to be unrecognised, 10 per cent of urban schools
and 16 per cent of rural schools functioning in premises smaller than 1,000sq.ft
(93m²), with 57 per cent of the teachers being untrained, and 67 per cent of them
being paid less than Rs.2,000 a month.

Private school clientele

In their 2006 study, Muralidharan & Kremer found that though the parents of children attending private schools were more educated and possessed a higher level of
assets,

> 'the absolute level of education of the parents of the children attending private
> schools is actually quite low. For instance, 20 per cent of the private school
> students are first-generation learners, which while lower than the 30 per cent
> in public schools, is still quite significant. Thus while private schools cater to
> the better off in the rural areas, many of their students come from disadvan-
> taged backgrounds. This is consistent with the results of Tooley and Dixon
> (2003) who mention that the majority of private schools in India cater to the
> poor (though their observation is based on an urban study)...'

A survey conducted by the Centre for Civil Society (in 2007) found that:

- 14 per cent of children from socio-economic class (SEC) C, D, E households sent
  their children to private-recognised schools;

- 28 per cent of children from SEC C households sent their children to private-
  recognised schools; and

- 14 per cent of children from SEC C households go to private Hindi-medium
  schools.

Note: The SECs – socio-economic classes – for this study were defined as being:

> C = petty trader who has completed his/her high school
>
> D = petty trader with up to four years of school education only
>
> E = illiterate person

Interestingly, this survey also found the following:

- Of the 95 per cent of government schoolteachers who had children in schools or
  colleges, 37 per cent were sending their children to private schools.

Why the poor choose private schools

With millions of parents making the choice of paying for their children to attend
private school even in a context where relatively lower cost or even free government

education is available, the reason is fairly obvious. As the PROBE report (1999) pointed out:

- Poor parents perceive the quality of the private schools to be higher than that of government schools;
- This is not restricted to perception, and the quality is actually higher in terms of:
  - level of teaching activity and time spent on teaching
  - higher levels of teacher activity and closer attention to students; and
- The greater accountability of private schools to parents also results in better quality of education.

In the process documentation of EQUIP, a programme to bring about quality improvement in a group of low-fee private schools in UP, Catholic Relief Services (2006) lists the following reasons articulated by parents for sending children to private schools:

1. Government schools often have insufficient teachers posted to them.
2. If teachers have indeed been posted, they are often absent, with the most quoted reason being their involvement in supporting 'administrative' duties.
3. The dysfunctional nature of the government school is also visible in poor daily attendance rates. [Recent surveys have put daily student attendance rates in government schools in UP as being below 60 per cent.] The poor quality of education in these schools and the need to supplement family incomes, e.g. by working in the fields, keeps students away. Consequently, parents who are willing to make the effort to educate their children conclude that such a school is not for their children.
4. Private schools also offer a scholarship of Rs.300 per annum (from the Social Welfare Board) for a percentage of children, which lures parents. Schools also admit a number of children for free or adjust the fees against the scholarship amount when it does come.

Professor Tooley, in his study 'Serving the needs of the poor: the private education sector in developing countries' (2001) also notes the existence of 'a significant number of scholarships – that is, free places for even poorer students. The free places were allocated by the School Correspondent on the basis of claims of need checked informally in the community. Five of the schools had between 15 and 20 per cent of students in free school places.'

Apart from the economics of demand and supply, Mehta (2005) points out that yet another reason for the demand for these schools is that they are popularly known as 'English-medium' schools, and it is this that attracts parents.

Case studies

Background

In order to study the situation of a small set of low-fee private schools, the authors selected clusters of schools located largely in two areas of Uttar Pradesh (UP). As India's largest state, as well as among those considered the least developed educationally, UP is critical to India's universalisation efforts.

Schools in two kinds of settings were observed and analysed. The first, in rural areas, were located around 35–42km from Lucknow, the state capital. The second set was located in a peri-urban area in the National Capital Region, near an industrial township. Apart from observation visits, interviews with a cross section of stakeholders and analysis of available documents were relied upon.

Rural schools

School profile

Four rural schools were visited, 35–42km away from Lucknow. The schools were established from 1974–2007. Although each of these villages had government schools, they also had a large number of private schools.

All schools, whether private or government, were located in close proximity, often being adjacent or just across the street from one another. Clearly, there had been migration from the government to the private schools. School managers also reported that a large number of students were still enrolled in the government school, and drew entitlements (such as uniform, scholarships or books, and at times also meals) from there. (Although the researchers could not gather data on the exact extent of this phenomenon, such dual enrolment is widely reported across the country, as cited elsewhere in this book.)

Private school principals and managers attribute the migration of students from government schools to theirs to repeated/regular absence of government school-teachers, and because 'even when they come, they do not teach' since they have a permanent job (i.e. a lifetime appointment). This was apparent as the researchers passed the government schools. One manager pointed out how the government

Table 4.1 Rural village schools

Village	Government schools	Private schools	Reported attendance in government schools
Tikaitganj	4	10	Poor
Niguar	1	2	Poor
Rewan seewan	1	4	Good
Sansanwar	3	7	Poor

schoolteachers in the school opposite his school arrived two hours late (since the bus from Lucknow arrived at that time) and left well before school ended (again, to synchronise with the bus timings).

The private schools were all individually owned, with the owner (often called the 'manager') appointing a principal to run the school. Owners had an education up to class 12 or a Bachelor's degree (BA), while the principal's education was usually BA or a Master's degree (MA), graduate or postgraduate.

All schools, except one, were to receive government 'recognition' soon after the time of writing. Only one school had classes up to primary, while others had up to class 10, either in one location or in the form of a 'branch' nearby.

The admission fee charged in the schools was Rs.50 per month, with only the most remote one not charging any admission fee. The monthly fee for primary-elementary classes was Rs.30–35, while for classes 9 and 10 it was Rs.60. No other fees were charged through the year.

The schools run from 7.30/8.00am to 1.00pm, with fewer holidays than government schools (to demonstrate that they are 'different' from government schools). In fact, the private schools claim to be working for as many as 280 days per annum; government school officially have only 220–240 days, of which they actually function for around 180 days or less (due to various reasons).

Infrastructure

In terms of space and facilities, the private schools had the absolute minimum. Three categories of infrastructure could be seen: rooms, thatched structures with no walls and open-air space. All spaces were narrow and congested. Where there were rooms, they had been crudely put together (i.e. unplastered bricks joined with mud). Every inch was covered with tables/benches or mats, children sitting elbow to el-bow, with no space to move about. These rooms were about as wide as a (narrow) corridor would be, with poor ventilation and low lighting. The sheds had no walls, being supported on bamboo/brick pillars, but were equally congested. Open-air space was not really available (i.e. space for children to play outside). Two of the schools had small, open-air classroom space only. During the rain, these classes cannot be held. No toilets were in evidence, though all owners claimed that they were 'under construction'.

The private schools were not really 'compounds' – rather they existed more as a collection of rooms/spaces not necessarily connected with each other, with rooms having been constructed as and when money came in. Hence, no boundary walls/gates were visible in any school, with one or two rooms being an extension of the owner's house.

On the whole, though, children did not display any discomfort. It is likely they have no expectations/experience of better infrastructure.

A few charts and books could be seen, although none of the schools had a library. One school had a computer, which staff claimed to use with children; however, it was quite obvious that this was more of a 'selling point' rather than something for actual use. Interestingly, none of the schools had electricity, with the computer being placed in a room in the owner's house adjacent to the school.

Appearances attract enrolment

In the running of the private schools, a background in education or any other real competence in the field is not considered important. On being asked his qualifications in a routine manner, one of the principals-cum-managers informed the researchers that he failed in his grade 12 exams and consequently opened the school the next year.

One clear impression was that since there is a great deal of competition among private schools, it is more important for them to *appear* to be good schools or at least to acquire the reputation, rather than actually *being* good schools. The school signboard unfailingly emphasises how it is an 'English-medium' school (irrespective of the fact that no teacher can speak/understand English). A building and a gate, where affordable, testify to the 'solidity' of the school. 'Trappings' that would classify these as schools are strategically displayed – a chart or two above the principal's chair, thick registers on the desks (with most pages blank), the computer mentioned earlier, a few teaching aids and the like. There was little evidence of these trappings actually being put to use – education is actually being *staged*. Schools use some of the above devices to distinguish themselves from the competition. Indeed, some of the managers of the visited schools were emphatic that the visit of the researchers would show the public that their school was better 'since it is being visited by outsiders.'

Students

The private schools had student populations ranging from 250–650, which was easily more than the daily attendance in any government school nearby. Where the school taught only up to primary level, the number of students was around 250. Only in one school was the number of boys and girls equal, while in others, the number of boys was much greater. Except in the nursery class, boys and girls were seated separately. A typical class had only one section, with 30–40 students. As a whole, schools had teacher-pupil ratios from 1:40 to 1:50.

Children came from families considered to have low socio-economic status – mainly poor and marginalised sections, including those from scheduled castes, illiterate/uneducated and/or minority communities (mainly Muslim).

Without exception, the capacity of the target population to pay the fees was low to very low.

Teachers

Private schools had between 5–15 teachers, typically one for 40–50 students. In all such schools, the ratio of female teachers was marginally higher than in government schools and one of the managers stated that they preferred to have more female teachers since this leads to better teacher retention; parents are also more comfortable sending girl children to school if there are female teachers. Teachers usually have a higher secondary education (i.e. class 12), with only one or two teachers having completed a college degree (BA). There was no teacher with any professional qualification or pre-service training. Nor are teachers oriented in any way: and just start teaching from the day they join a school.

The salaries low-fee private school teachers are paid can only be described as inhuman. Most teachers are paid Rs.500–800/month, a few are paid Rs.800–1,000 and only one teacher was found to be paid Rs.1,500. Unemployment being so high among the educated, getting teachers to work at this rate (below minimum wage, which is Rs.100/day for unskilled labour as per government notification) is not difficult. Teachers also feel that they are gaining some experience (if not money) rather than sitting idle (they would not take up wage labour since they are 'educated'). One motivation for teachers is that their experience might help them in the selection tests conducted by the state Public Service Commission, which need to be cleared by any aspirant for a stable government job. For teachers, therefore, work in such schools is merely a stepping-stone to other opportunities and there is naturally a very high turnover rate. This also results in a fair proportion of teachers being new and inexperienced, and therefore cheaply available.

There is no real 'contract' between teacher and school, and neither party needs to give any notice for termination. This leaves teachers vulnerable to being dismissed at any time. Schools can deal with turnover without much difficulty, since there are always many educated unemployed persons available; thus, the situation is definitely weighted against the teacher in many ways.

This surplus of teachers is not likely to dry up for quite some time to come. This is because the general unemployment rate in India is very high. Those with 10–12 years of education do not wish to work in agriculture, wage labour or skilled labour and do not have access to vocational/technical education. Hence the market is full of a large number of unemployed youth on the lookout for experience, if not actual work/jobs. At the same time many states, such as Karnataka, have far too many trained teachers (who have been through pre-service courses), but insufficient jobs in government schools – which have a higher salary and far better employment terms. The annual government schoolteacher intake in this state would be in the region of 8,000 (less in some years), while the supply of newly-trained would-be teachers is around 60,000–80,000.

Education/classroom 'processes'

Children's attendance in private low-fee schools varies greatly on a daily basis, ranging from 50–90 per cent. In one school, a large number of the children were absent since they had to be present the next day in clean uniform for the Independence Day function (15 August) and, having only one set of clothes, they were washing them that day.

There is no concept of a clear curriculum or syllabus, with only the textbooks serving as a means of determining what needs to be done. Textbooks from local private publishers are used in private schools. Unlike in government schools, children are required to buy these textbooks, which strain the budget of these families. (Private textbook publishers provide many incentives to these schools for 'selecting' their textbooks.) The only exception is in class 5, for maths and Hindi; here, government school textbooks are used since children appear for the government school board examination at the end of class 5.

Teaching is not always very structured, with there being only a loose timetable that is often not adhered to. Teachers enter the class and start teaching from wherever the lesson had been left off previously. 'Teaching' usually means lecturing/'explaining' the lesson, with little scope for ensuring that all children have followed what is going on. Homework is given and even 'seen' (if not corrected), though there is usually no family help available to children at home. The high turnover of teachers also prevents any continuity through the year.

A major emphasis is on 'discipline', with corporal punishment being meted out to both boys and girls.

Relations with parents, community

The private schools in the case study try to organise quarterly (and in one case monthly) meetings with parents, though often it is school issues that are discussed rather than children's progress, and attendance is usually poor. There are some instances of community contribution in the form of a fan or a couple of chairs having been donated to the school. As one principal said, however, 'That they send children to our school, is their contribution.'

The economics of a low-fee private school

Though the monthly fee is about as low as it is possible to charge (it amounts to less than half of a day's minimum wage fixed for unskilled labour), the levels of poverty are such that many families are unable to pay, at least not regularly. In a typical month, the fees may come in for only around half the children. That is, if 600 students are enrolled, only around 300–400 will pay the fees. There is also a charitable disposition, and students who are unable to pay the fees tend to be treated a little more kindly than in the government school – as they come from 'our own community'.

Since there are government provisions for scholarships for poor students (Rs.300/ year for primary students, and Rs.480 for those in higher classes), the schools try hard to obtain as many of these as possible. The scholarship money comes direct to the school; they deduct the fee and pass on the remainder to the family. Often this might amount to a relatively large sum coming in one go, say Rs.5,000 for around 10 children who have been taught free for a whole year. This source of income compensates the schools somewhat. Such scholarships are not always sure, however, and schools pursue them vigorously throughout much of the year (often government schools are given preference over private schools, and it is as much 'networking' as merit that results in securing the scholarships).

Vacations are yet another source of income. Both government and private schools have only about a month's vacation during summer, and break during winter as well. Fees are taken from children during this period, although teachers' salaries are not paid during this time (especially during the summer vacation).

Typically, for 600 children there are around nine teachers. The salary of three will be a little higher (Rs.800–1,000 per month), five being paid between Rs.500–800, with the manager him/herself getting around Rs.1,000 per month. Schools also spend Rs.5,000–10,000 for maintenance, repair etc. annually (the building is so poorly made that it needs this). Managers also take a fee from the teachers they send for in-service training conducted anywhere. All-in-all, around Rs.2,000 is saved per month, and Rs.5,000–7,000 during the summer months.

This is not always sufficient as an economic motive, since a skilled labourer could earn more. However, there is a notion of 'dignity' attached to running a school, something 'educated' and 'civilised' that is accorded higher status. Many of the schools are opened by those of 'higher' or more 'powerful' castes who would find it difficult to take up wage labour/small business such as shopkeeping since that is considered to be of low status; indeed, they can take up such opportunities only if they migrate to other areas, such as cities. Neither do they have the skills or resources other than their social position, and setting up a school provides an avenue that 'saves face' and even builds on the legitimacy of their social standing, despite a complete lack of professional background in education.

There is another motivation for those who start these schools – it is the opportunity to become the 'owners of a large building' over a period of time. In the beginning when the school is unknown, it tends to have fewer students and limited inflow of money. Rooms are thus built over a period of time, as and when the money comes in. So while school owners may not earn much money, they do become owners of a building(s) over a period of time, depending on how 'successful' the school is (measured in numbers of students and the years it has run without closing down).

Finally, owners also hope that one day theirs will become a 'recognised' school and the government will make them a semi-aided/aided institution, which will then fund their requirements (except the building).

Peri-urban schools

School profile

Three schools were seen in the National Capital Region of Delhi. School 1 was located in an urban residential area; schools 2 and 3 were in urban villages, with school 2 being in an unauthorised residential area (with very inferior living conditions, but not yet declared a slum) next to a 'posh'/more upmarket area. School 3 was a little more remote, being located in a peri-urban area, not yet touched by the 'modernity' visible in other parts; most people here commute daily to upper-/middle-income areas to work as domestic help/wage labour. All schools were around 20–30km from central Delhi. School 1 has children from a middle-class background, with the accompanying 'push' to go to school. School 2 has children from poor families, a majority working as domestic and support staff in the houses in the richer area.

Though there are other government schools in the region, urban and peri-urban areas appear to be less well serviced by the government school system than rural areas. (This is partly due to the greater emphasis on rural areas in the two major countrywide primary and elementary education programmes of the GoI, i.e. the District Primary Education Programme (DPEP) and SSA).

As in the rural areas, low-fee private schools in urban and peri-urban areas are individually owned (as contrasted with the high-fee private schools that are usually trust owned).

School 1 (Noida Sector 19)

From among all the schools observed, this urban low-fee school came the closest to approximating the high-fee private school. Established in 1987, the school is managed by a couple (but owned by the husband), and a principal has been appointed (since the government directive is that the owner cannot be the principal). The school has been recognised by the government and has classes from grades 1 to 12.

The school charges an admission fee of Rs.150, along with a monthly fee of Rs.400. This might appear higher compared to other areas, but would be considered low-fee in this context: regular private schools charging in the range of Rs.1,500–Rs.5,000 per month in this area while those considered high-end charging over Rs.10,000–25,000 per month.

The school hours are from 8.30 am–1.45 pm, with the usual holidays as in other private schools. The total number of teaching days amounts to 180–200, again like other large private schools.

Infrastructure

The school has a large building, with sufficient indoor as well as outdoor space. This is considered an outward sign that the school is established and has been running for a long time. This school also started small; as in the case of rural schools, it added a little every year so that during the course of a decade an impressive property has been created.

All classes have a room to themselves (in rural schools they often share a room) and the usual charts and teaching aids are visible in most rooms. Functional furniture (desks and chairs) is available in all rooms, and the school has seven computers, which are kept in a separate computer room.

The school has separate toilets for boys and girls, and its electricity connection is backed up by a power generator.

Students

The total number of students in the school is around 1,600 (with an almost even distribution of boys and girls), with there being three sections per class, and 40–50 students per section. Children come mainly from lower-middle-class families, with around 200 students (only boys) from lower-income groups and mixed ethnicities and castes. Parents send children here because the fee is lower than other private schools. The school also has a separate section for poorer children, where they teach in Hindi. Unlike rural schools, there are no reports of parents not paying fees or of any children being educated for free.

Teaching/classroom 'processes'

As in most other schools, the main classroom processes consist of explaining the lessons, doing exercises, with an occasional project (i.e. something made/done at home, and displayed in school). The curriculum followed is that of the Central Board of Secondary Education. The 'English medium' school essentially prescribes textbooks written in English, with a few words in the language being used now and then by teachers and children.

There is no reported interaction with parents on a regular basis.

Teachers

The school has 25 teachers, which leads to a teacher-pupil ratio of above 1:60. Teachers must be trained (i.e. possess pre-service training – either NTT [Nursery Teachers' Training] or B.Ed, MA /MSc for higher classes).

Teacher salaries are around Rs.2,000 – although they are required to sign on a higher amount, which gives the owners greater income tax relief. Teachers are not allowed to talk to each other during working hours! Asked why they teach in this school, answers included experience, money and to pass the time (since some teachers would have little else to do otherwise).

School 2 (Village Aggapur)

School 2 is an individually-owned school established in 2002 and is located in a peri-urban area. It is recognised by the government and has classes from grades 1 to 10. Beyond class 6, there are only a few children in each class. Rooms for classes 11 and 12 are under construction, after which the school will be extended to these classes.

The school fees are Rs.170 per month, with no admission fee being charged. However, Rs.20–30 per month is charged towards power back-up, toilet construction, furniture and other such expenses. Parents also pay up to Rs.100 per month for transport (by cycle rickshaw, since none of the low-fee private schools has a bus).

Infrastructure

While school 2 has a compound and a boundary wall, the quality of construction was very much like that of the rural schools. The owner lives in two rooms in the building, which is essentially narrow and congested, with very little space. There is a little outdoor space, rooms for all classes, and toilets. A power generator is available, paid for through the extra school fees.

Children sit on stools and tables in the classrooms, which have a few (dull) charts and pictures, inappropriately placed and certainly not used. The school has a computer (for older students), with a different class getting the opportunity to use it every day. Some of the classrooms also had a few books.

Students

The total number of students is around 400 in school 2. In class 4 (a typical primary class), there are 17 boys and 20 girls. Each class has one section, with 35–40 students in each. Students come from low-income families, whose monthly income would be around Rs.3,000–4,000 per month.

Teachers

With eight teachers in the school, the teacher-pupil ratio is around 1:40 to 1:50.

Teachers seemed to be teaching regularly in school 2, with some impact on students (in terms of their ability to respond and awareness of what was being taught). Few of the children have resources or support at home. Parent interviews revealed satisfaction with teachers.

Students revealed that some of them take extra tuition (from tutors in the neighbourhood or teachers from the school), especially in terms of help with homework, and this supplements the salaries of teachers somewhat.

School 3 (Village Surajpur, UP)

School 3 is located in an urban village and caters to the population located in a single, large habitation. It was much worse off than schools 1 and 2 in terms of infrastructure. It had even less parental involvement in children's education, since most working adults had to commute long distances daily for work and did not have the time/resources to focus on their children's education.

In most other respects, school 3 was closer to the rural schools – it was marginally better than they were, but much worse off than school 2.

Although there is much variation in the backgrounds/locations of these private schools, they all share the same shortcomings. While the buildings and their design are very similar (they do not even have the cosmetic appearance of being a school, looking as they do like any other structure), their other shortcomings (and strengths) are similar.

For the poorest parents who face enormous financial hardships and make desperate efforts to send a child to school, it is the extras that pinch hard, such as the spending on transport (cycle rickshaws packed with children are not very safe or reliable), uniforms etc. In the urban areas the schools are able to insist on uniforms, whereas in rural areas parents are often too poor to be able to afford school wear and schools are unable to enforce this rule.

In rural areas, schools are smaller, closer to each other and compete with one another much more aggressively. At the same time, they also tend to have an informal alliance, wherein they avoid taking steps to deliberately/unnecessarily affect the others' business (such as opening a branch near a flourishing school).

Interviews

Two parents of children in schools 2 and 3 in the peri-urban areas were interviewed, a father from the first and a mother from the second. In terms of occupation, income and social background they represent the typical parent who sends their children to low-fee schools. Their views, too, represent the considerations that lie behind school choice.

Interview with parent (father of child in school 2)

Both the mother and father of the child are illiterate and have never studied in school. The father works as an odd-job man, taking whatever work is available – from working as gardener, guard and rickshaw puller, to mason, or house painter, with occasional tailoring work. His wife works as a domestic help. The family income adds up to around Rs.3,500/month. Being caretakers of a partly constructed house, they live in a shed in its backyard, which reduces their expenses.

The couple have three children, of which one child (a son) is not yet of school-going age. The younger daughter is enrolled in a school run by a religious organisation, while the older one was studying in class 4 in school 2. The children do not earn any income for their parents.

The father felt that in the government school children 'only sit around and no studies take place'. (He did not know where the nearest government school was). He originally put the older daughter in the religious organisation's school, because they provided free uniform, books and food for the first three years; he then moved her to school 2, and is going to do the same for the second daughter. In his opinion, the studies are not as good in the religious organisation's school – however, the child learns how to go school, gets used to the routine, learns how to 'sit' in the class; in any case, how much do children learn at this age, he feels. So given the free provisions, it is fine to start at the religious school. Later, when the child is, according to him, ready to learn, then the private school fee (Rs.170, which started at Rs.100) is worthwhile.

He feels the school is doing well; earlier there were not many children, but now it is 'full'. All subjects are taught. His daughter comes back home and works on her own, because no one in the family is literate and can help. Sometimes, his brother, who is a little educated, helps.

Interview with mother (parent of child in school 3)

Neither parent is literate, never having been to school. The family income is around Rs.4,000 per month. The couple have four children. The oldest daughter, 17 years old, dropped out of school very early and now works full-time as a domestic help. The second daughter, around 15, studied up to class 5; she works full-time as domestic help with the mother. Her third daughter was recently moved from private school to a government school (because her husband had stopped working and they found it difficult to raise money for the fees). Her youngest child, now in school 3, is about to be moved to the government school (because the child (a son) had not learnt to read or write at age 9, and she saw no point in spending any more money).

Because she was not at home much of the day, due to her work as domestic help in many houses, she was not able to supervise the children or even be sure if they attended school regularly; this was another reason for putting them into government school, where 'it does not matter if they do not attend every day'. She leaves home at 7am, earlier than the children leave for school, and her son in particular often misses school.

She said, 'The quality of teaching or how well teachers teach depends on whose child it is. Teachers pay attention to those who are better off or whose father has some power or if the person is socially known to them. When it comes to our children, they don't bother....'

Although this mother does think of her children's education, she is unable to separate it from other issues that bother her such as the unsafe environment in the village, especially for girls and women, her husband not having/taking up work, and the slow transition of her family into an unhappy one.

In urban areas, it is men who tend to lose their jobs more frequently and to be without work, mainly because even if domestic work were available, they would not be able to take it up. There are few other employment opportunities. Thus, this off-on employment of the low-income urban/peri-urban father tends to affect the child's enrolment/continuation in private schools.

In urban areas, expenses on education are also greater in terms of uniforms, books and stationery, transport, school demands (for different facilities provided such as toilets, power back-up, computers etc.), private tuition and the like. This has its own role to play when deciding whether a child's education is 'worth it'.

Interview with child (student in school 2)

This child, a student in class 4, was the oldest daughter of the parent interviewed for school 2.

This was her fourth year in the school. She enjoyed being in this school, and especially being with her friends (she did not have friends around her home, since the family lived as caretakers of a partly constructed house in a higher-income residential area). She also felt that the lessons were good in the school and that the teachers teach well. What she did not like was the corporal punishment. Beatings of both boys and girls by teachers and the principal are common. They are also told to stand with their hands up for a long time and 'half the children are scared all the time'. The school is also strict about rules such as wearing uniforms (children without school wear are turned away).

The child does not have any help with her homework and does it herself. In fact, there is plenty of homework to be done, even during vacations. When asked if they are taught in English (since this claimed to be an English-medium school), she said that no one speaks English, only a few words are used.

Supply and quality issues

The 'worth' of government education

In the survey conducted by the Centre for Civil Society (2007), the respondents were asked:

- Based on the quality of education, infrastructure and facilities etc. available in the school, if you have to pay for it from your pocket, what would you be willing to pay for government school education?

On average, parents are willing to pay nearly Rs.66 for a government school.

To the second question:

- How much do you think the government is spending per child per month on education?

Most parents felt that the government spends around Rs.100 per child, nearly 37 per cent feeling that government spending was around Rs.50!

The study estimates that in reality government schools cost taxpayers 'on a conservative estimate, Rs.800) per month per child! Government school education is valued by its consumers at less than one eighth of what it costs the exchequer. The discord between the perceived value of government schools and the actual value is indicative of the quality of the education provided. Rs.800 has not translated into quality worthy of that amount for the consumer.'

How much are people willing to pay?

What people actually pay for education in low-fee private schools, though, is very different from the perceived value of government schools. Unfortunately, little information or research is available on the actual fees charged by private schools in different areas. The Centre for Civil Society (2007) survey quoted above found the following:

- The average fees charged by the private primary schools surveyed was Rs.241 per month[3];

- 42 per cent of them were charging fees between Rs.100 and Rs.200 per month;

- 45 per cent of the parents of children studying in government schools mentioned that they had to spend money on private tuition; and

- On average, parents were spending nearly Rs.2,200 on private tuition and Rs.1,100 on transport per year for their child's education.

In the case studies included in this chapter, it can be seen that the fees range from Rs.30 to Rs.400 depending on the area and the reputation of the school.

The quality of private school education

Given the investment that parents make into private school education, what are the 'returns' they obtain? Although the 'better quality' of private schools might be intuited, claims that this equals better quality **education** are difficult to substantiate since there is no commonly agreed upon set of indicators of education (as a holistic development of the child). Most claims to quality are limited to comparison of scholastic performance in cognitive or subject-based tests, with the scores being used as a proxy for quality of education. It is within this limitation that the following research is presented.

School Observations
Three government (primary) schools
Schools observed in: Chitrakoot, Barabanki and Auraiya districts

Main observations:

- New infrastructure was visible in all the schools in the form of new school buildings that had replaced old ones. In one school, the school grounds had a newly-built kitchen for the midday meal, which is now an entitlement for all children, though it was not in use since it had neither doors nor water.
- Toilets were in a deplorable condition.
- The school registers showed high enrolment, although the number of children actually present in the schools was found to be much fewer.
- In two out of the three government schools visited, the number of staff posted was three, but there was only one teacher present. All children from classes 1–5 sat in one classroom. The teacher was found to be 'minding' the students, rather than teaching them.
- The one teacher present was usually the *Siksha Mitra* (or the community/'para' teacher, who is less qualified and paid much less than the regular teacher).
- Other than the *Shiksha Mitra*, no other teacher prepared TLM (teaching-learning material). No teaching material (other than textbooks) was used in the higher classes (though there is a separate grant for purchase of TLM and in-service training emphasises its use).
- The concept of a 'period' or break between lessons was not followed in the schools. In one school visited, the school time was divided into pre-lunch and post-lunch sessions, with one subject being taught pre-lunch and another post-lunch.
- Children did not seem to know what lesson was being taught to them in any of the schools observed.
- Teachers used the cane regularly on children.
- A total of 20 days' in-service training in a year was earmarked for all teachers. In practice, however, on average a teacher underwent 8–12 days of training in a year. During the trainings, teachers were taught how to prepare a lesson plan. In practice, however, they did not prepare such plans.
- The schools were periodically evaluated by the *nyaya panchayat* (the local self-government body), which assigned a grade to the schools. No one (not the teachers, principal nor the Block Resource Centre Co-ordinator) seemed to know what grade had been assigned to the schools being observed, which included a government primary school located on the same campus as a Block Resource Centre.

Source: Catholic Relief Services, 2006.

The study 'Mobilising the Private Sector for Public Education', co-sponsored by the World Bank Kennedy School of Government, Harvard University (2005) points out that with schools being affiliated to different examination boards (each with its own curricula and examinations), learning achievement data across school types and states does not exist. Hence:

> 'school effectiveness studies in India are based on small surveys of schools in individual states, rather than on nationwide or even state-wide data....Thus,

studies of the relative effectiveness of public and private schools in India have had to rely on standardised achievement tests carried out by the researchers themselves in small samples of schools. These studies have been carried out in different parts of India (Tamil Nadu, Madhya Pradesh, Uttar Pradesh and Andhra Pradesh, respectively) but they share the common conclusion that private school students outperform their public school counterparts even after controlling for the schools' student intakes'.

As mentioned above, the study by Tooley (2005b) in North Shahadara (Delhi) tested around 3,500 children in mathematics and English, and 'found that children in unrecognised private schools on an average scored 72 per cent higher in mathematics than government school students, 83 per cent higher in Hindi and 246 per cent higher in English.'

In his study of the unrecognised schools of Punjab, Mehta (2005) analysed examination results in terminal grades 5 and 7. While the overall 'pass' percentage was similar across recognised and unrecognised schools, the percentage of children scoring 60 per cent and above was higher in the case of the latter.

Kingdon's (1996a, 1996b) study researched in some detail the question: 'Is the popularity of private fee-charging schools in India to be explained by their superior quality?' This compared the three types of schools – private-unaided, private-aided and government schools – in urban Lucknow, in the state of Uttar Pradesh. Data was collected from 902 students of grade 8 (13 to 14-years-old), in 30 schools from the three school categories. Kingdon also took measures to control for social and personal factors. The results were revealing, with the private-unaided students scoring almost twice as highly as the government and private-aided schools in both mathematics and reading (on the raw scores). This edge diminished somewhat when the scores were corrected to account for social and personal factors, though it did remain statistically significant. For example, post correction, the private-unaided schools were still 27 per cent more effective at teaching mathematics than the other schools.

Some research questions

Given the size of the school system, research on the quality of low-fee private schools appears to have analysed a tiny proportion, though it does lend credence to the general notion that students get to 'study' more in private schools. Apart from greater research to confirm this, other questions need to be addressed:

- Do private schools really provide a greater 'value addition' to poor students compared to government schools, who have even poorer students and a greater proportion of first generation learners?

- How well do 'good' government schools perform when compared to 'good' low-fee private ones, especially if the overall quality of education is emphasised rather than scholastic achievement alone?

- If achievement tests are to be used as a proxy for quality, what kind of tests should really be used? At present, achievement tests (as well as school examinations) typically tend to focus on a limited number of lower-order, mechanistic learning objectives (e.g. spelling rather than expression). Thus, such tests seldom assess critical learning goals in subjects. So a question that might need addressing is: how would the comparative advantage of private schools alter if critical learning goals were properly assessed? (In recent research by the author, there is some indication that private schools might not have as strong an edge in such a case, since they tend to rely on rote memorisation and 'exam preparation' and might emerge to be as 'bad' as government schools).

- Finally, while private schools might 'score' when compared to those from a near-dysfunctional government school system, it is still worth exploring what the quality of these schools is *per se*.

School efficiency

Apart from test and examination results, another aspect of school quality is in terms of school efficiency. In her study of aided, unaided and government high schools of Mysore, Josephine (1999) identified patterns of resource usage that are likely to apply to schools in general. Her key findings indicated the following:

- Private institutions had lower unit costs when compared to government schools – 'they pay less to teachers, may operate shift systems, use teaching-aids, laboratories and libraries more efficiently.'

- Despite higher unit costs, government schools had lower outputs, as a result of greater wastage and stagnation. Unlike parents of children in private schools, parents of children in government schools took less care to ensure their children's attendance, and much higher dropout rates were observed in government schools.

- In terms of examination results, the pass percentage was the greatest in English-medium private schools (the least being in government schools). The English-medium schools also registered better marks, at a lower unit cost than in government schools (though, of course, the high private costs were not taken into account). Josephine also documents that students enrolled in higher performing schools came from higher socio-economic strata, and apart from having a better home environment, they also used private tuition in greater measure.

- Government schools made poor use of available resources (for example, poor maintenance of libraries) and funds (e.g. delays in purchase of lab equipment, leading to cost escalation and the school being deprived of the resource for the duration), thus failing to get 'optimum return for the money spent'.

The dynamics of opening and running private schools

The manner in which private schools open is as much a social as a business or administrative process. Catholic Relief Services (2006) in the documentation of EQUIP describes it in detail below:

- New private schools open in the villages all the time. The saying in the villages goes, new private schools open once the crop is cut and there is money to invest! Moreover, private textbook publishers provide incentives such as school furniture, blackboards etc. to these private schools, which make it easier for school managers to run the school. In return, private schools have to use the textbooks promoted by the publishers.

- School managers compete with each other in villages to enrol school-age children in their respective private schools.

- 'Recognised' school status helps to attract children. Benefits include government scholarship for children enrolled in a recognised private school, in addition to the implicit benefit of studying in a recognised school. However, 'recognised' school status does not come easily to these schools. Although the fee for applying for 'recognised' status is not very high, the 'commissions' (bribes) for processing the application are three to four times that amount. Moreover, the waiting-time before the school gets 'recognised' status is very long.

- The usual practice is for coaching schools (a private school normally opens initially as a coaching or tuition centre) to locate themselves adjacent to a government school. The students who study in these coaching or unrecognised private schools are those that are enrolled in the adjacent government school. In the government school, teacher absenteeism is high, so these children attend the coaching school. More importantly, government school children receive scholarships regularly because the money is routed through the *panchayat* (the local self government body). Further, parents understand that a coaching school is run purely with a commercial objective; hence they pay their children's tuition fees. In this way, coaching schools thrive in rural areas (eventually 'graduating' to being private schools).

Why private schools prefer to remain unrecognised

While private schools in some states (as in UP) seek recognition for the benefits such as government scholarships that it brings, in large parts of the country such schools appear to *prefer* not being recognised. Mehta (2005) points out that it 'is not mandatory to obtain permission from the local administration to open a school. It is rather strange to note that to open a grocery shop, some sort of permission/registration is needed but to open a school, no such permission is essential.'

Being 'unrecognised' allows schools to get away with paying teachers between one-fifth and one-tenth of government salary levels. Mehta observes that such schools 'avoid conditions laid by administration with reference to qualification, training and pay structure of teachers, curriculum, medium of instruction and textbooks.'

Fees and scholarships as major preoccupations

Once the school starts, scholarship and fee issues come into play, tending to remain on-stage for much of the year. Catholic Relief Services (2006) captures the yearly drama in the extensive extract below:

'Parents and private school managers compete with each other for the scholarship money that the government provides for children's education. Children are the worst sufferers of this tussle between parents and private school managers, which unfolds as follows:

- Teachers' salary in the private schools is dependent on fees received from children. Around 50 per cent of the students are unable to pay school fees due to economic reasons. Only in very small parts of the state is this percentage a little better at 30 per cent.

- Parents pay the school fees regularly for a few months, and then reach a point when they are unable to pay. So they wait for the government scholarship to pay up, which sometimes takes up to three years to come. The scholarship amount that the child finally receives is for one year and not three years. When the scholarship money does come, it is sent to the parents via the school address. Negotiations then take place between the parents and the school over how this money is divided. The parents seek to be reimbursed for the fees they have actually paid whilst the school seeks to be reimbursed for the fees they waived. As the money received is usually not sufficient to cover both, this involves a fair deal of bargaining on both sides. The school thus receives fees for fewer months than the child actually attends.

- More than parents, it is in the interest of private schools to follow-up with the government on the yearly scholarship money due to the school children when it is delayed. This is because it is out of this money that teachers' salaries have to be paid, since parents will often fail to pay school fees regularly.

- Invariably, private school managers end up paying huge commissions (bribes) at different levels of government to obtain the scholarship money. Despite this, only a few influential school managers succeed. The remaining private schools that fail in their efforts to organise the scholarship money are forced to drop the names of defaulting children (who have not paid school fees) from the school register. Consequently, school enrolment falls and the management is unable to pay teachers' salaries; the result is that teachers begin to leave.

- Often parents themselves remove their children from the school when the scholarship money arrives (which is usually for a year), especially if their children's school fees are overdue by more than a year. In such situations, parents prefer to put their children in another school, as they are unable to pay the school fees for the period beyond one year and all in one go. The same story repeats itself in the new school into which the child is admitted.

- Sometimes a "personal} relationship with a school manager influences parents' decisions regarding school choice. Often a child is withdrawn from a school if a parent's friend opens a school in the village. The child is admitted to this friend's school, the "friend" normally being someone who loans money to the family during times of need.'

Subsistence-level education

As may be gathered from the sections above, education in low-fee private schools is essentially 'subsistence-level' education and a preoccupation with economic survival permeates all activities in such schools. One very visible reflection of this is in the background of teachers and the salaries paid to them. In his study of 878 unrecognised private schools in 13 blocks of Haryana, Aggarwal (2000) observed that teachers were, in general, unqualified and poorly paid and had received no training.

The situation of teachers in Tamil Nadu, a state ranked much higher on the Educational Development Index (EDI) than Haryana, was not much better. The SV Chittibabu Commission (2003) found nearly 23 per cent of private schools to be unrecognised, with 57 per cent of the teachers being untrained and 67 per cent of these being paid less than Rs.2,000 a month.

In Uttar Pradesh, ranked nearly at the bottom of the EDI, teacher salaries may be as low as Rs.600–800, which is simply not enough to meet day-to-day needs. This naturally leads to high turnover of teachers in such schools. Interestingly, in one of the schools visited by Catholic Relief Services (2006) the teacher turnover was low 'because teachers of this school long ago invested in the school; financial investments were made toward 'aided school' status from the government, which is yet to come. These teachers are, therefore, not likely to leave the school.'

Studies such as the PROBE report (1999), the Pratichi Trust Report (2002) and Pratham's ASER (2005) report that the low cost of hiring teachers in rural private schools (who are often paid just one fifth of what government schoolteachers are) allows these schools to 'pass on' the savings thus made to parents through low fees.

In their study on teacher absence in India, Kremer et al (2004), compared teacher absenteeism in government versus private schools. Some of their key findings were as follows:

- 25 per cent of teachers were absent from school, and only about half were teaching, during unannounced visits to a nationally representative sample of government primary schools in India;

Low-cost Private Education

- Teachers in private schools and contract teachers, who face very different incentives, have similar or lower absence rates while being paid a fraction of government teachers' salaries;

- Regular teachers in rural government schools typically get paid about three to eight times more than their counterparts in rural private schools; and

- Private schoolteachers are only slightly less likely to be absent than public schoolteachers in general, but are 8 percentage points less likely to be absent than public schoolteachers in the same village. This is because private schools are disproportionately located in villages with particularly high absence rates in government schools.

School Observations
Two private (primary) schools
Schools observed in Hardoi and Deoria districts

Main Observations:

- Of the two schools visited, one was a 'recognised' school while the other one was not.

- Children's enrolment had come down in both the schools over the years (from 250 to 140 students in a period of five years, and 300 to 110 students in a period of 10 years for school 1 and school 2 respectively). In one case, this was due to the opening of a government junior school in the village.

- School attendance was 50 per cent for school 1 and 90 per cent for school 2 on the day of the school visits.

- The school fees varied between Rs.15 to Rs.20 in the two schools.

- Children enrolled in the schools belonged to all caste categories.

- Classes were held in the open due to the lack of an adequate school building.

- Textbooks from local private publishers were used in the schools, except for class 5 math and Hindi textbooks, which were government school textbooks. This is because after reaching grade 5, children appeared for government school board examinations. Children had to purchase these textbooks, which placed an economic burden on the parents.

- In one school, only boys had been provided with desks and benches. Girls in the same class sat on the ground.

- Teachers' salaries depended on the regular payment of school fees, and there were fewer teachers where students had failed to pay school fees. As a result, the remaining teachers had to manage more than one class in these schools.

- The concept of a 'period' or break between lessons was not followed in the schools.

- Teachers were untrained.

- Teachers carried a cane all the time. Discussions with children revealed that they were regularly punished in the age-old ways: Boys become *'murgha'* (cock), and are made to crouch on the ground, head between their legs, to remain in that position for a long time. Girls became *'kursi'* (chair); they are made to stand with bent knees for long periods.

Source: Catholic Relief Services (2006)

While the poor functioning of the government school system is apparent in such information, the study also points to the possibility that 'the entry of private schools leads to the exit of politically-influential families from the public school system, and further weakens pressure on public schoolteachers to attend school.'

A study by De et al (2002b), in UP, Bihar and Rajasthan found that the new private schools fared no better than the dilapidated government schools. The little extra space in the school manager's house served as the school, and children were cramped into dingy, small rooms. Being a recognised school made it no better, and such schools had no teaching aids or other facilities such as a library. 'If at all there was a playground, it was the 10 feet by 10 feet (9m²) courtyard of the house. Very few schools had trained teachers. The state of the unrecognised schools was even worse.'

In their survey of private provision in eight states, Mehrotra and Parthasarathi (2006) found that the 'new neo-liberal mantra' of private sector education does not contribute to gender and social equity. 'Despite their better physical facilities, their teachers are poorly paid and trained; and although their outcome and process indicators are better than for government schools, they remain unregulated and offer a poor alternative to low-quality government schools.'

Improving the quality of low-fee private schools

Many advocates of the low-fee private school tend to ignore a crucial aspect – the fact that the bad is being chosen over the worse does not make it good! Before such schools offer a worthwhile education, considerable effort needs to be made to improve their overall quality. One such effort that worked at improving the quality of around 100 low-fee private schools in UP has been EQUIP (the Educational Quality Improvement Programme) supported by Catholic Relief Services (2006). EQUIP organised schools in clusters wherein resources could be shared, and developed indicators for quality (in consultation with teachers and managers) that were rolled out in a phased manner, with development of teacher and manager capacity alongside. Over the years 2001–2006 a transformation was witnessed in these schools. While the physical environment improved greatly, classroom processes become more active and greater learner involvement was visible. Enrolment (and therefore the revenues) in these schools surged, which enabled sustainability and growth, even though the fees charged were no more than those in neighbouring schools. A comparative study of the learning levels attained in EQUIP schools versus non-EQUIP, low-fee private schools is underway, and preliminary analysis of results indicates that children in EQUIP schools outperform their counterparts in other schools on a range of indicators. Interestingly, this programme does not appear to have required a heavy investment. In EQUIP's documentation, it is noted that the 'EQUIP budget per child per year works out to Rs.700. With this low budget, EQUIP seems to have made significant changes in the schools covered by it....'

An unanticipated outcome was the degree of community support that EQUIP generated. For example, given the lack of space for group work, most of the EQUIP schools opted for outdoor seating. For around two months a year, children and teachers were affected by strong winds, prompting the community to discuss with management the possibility of a good school building with adequate space. Parents were also willing to pay higher school fees in such cases.

On occasion, the community has demonstrated its support even more strongly. Catholic Relief Services study (2006) points out the example of Chitrakoot cluster, 'where parents of a cluster school stood their ground in the face of pressures from a competing new private school whose influential school manager insisted parents remove their wards from this cluster school, and instead send them to his non-cluster school. The parents who had begun to relate to EQUIP and the education quality benefits it delivered, fought for their children to remain in the cluster school.'

Impact on the system

Given the scale of growth, the impact of the burgeoning private school sector may be felt on the government education system on at least five fronts, the last two being 'softer' though equally critical areas. These five areas are detailed in the sections below.

Declining enrolment in the government system

The poor, who constitute by far the largest group in India, are voting with their feet and meagre resources against the government education system. The impact of this can be seen in the slowing down of the growth of the system. As the table below shows, in 180 districts in 2005–06 *enrolment in government schools is declining*. This represents over a quarter of India's total 604 districts. Most states appear to be facing this situation, and the number of states thus affected has increased the last three years. A decline in the growth rate of child population does not explain the phenomenon, given the number of children who are still out of school. Kerala, the state ranked the highest in the Education Development Index in India, has actually been forced to close down schools across a number of districts for lack of demand.

Subsidies to private sector and duplication eat into government resources

In his paper 'Public Subsidies in Education in India', Tilak discusses the subsidies given to private (aided) schools, a sector that has grown over the last decade:

'There is a large private sector in education, which receives state support. Subsidies to such private institutions include both explicit subsidies and implicit subsidies. Implicit subsidies take the form of provision of land at concessional prices, tax exemptions on income and tax exemptions on material used for the

Table 4.2 Number of districts where enrolment in classes 1 to 5 in government schools declined over the previous year

State/Union Territory	2003–04	2004–05	2005–06
Andhra Pradesh	22	14	20
Assam	2	2	4
Bihar	12	1	9
Chandigarh	–	1	0
Chhattisgarh	3	6	7
Delhi	–	–	3
Gujarat	8	12	1
Haryana	6	7	12
Himachal Pradesh	11	6	12
Jammu & Kashmir	–	–	2
Jharkhand	3	3	1
Karnataka	17	21	25
Kerala	9	8	0
Madhya Pradesh	14	3	7
Maharashtra	14	26	1
Meghalaya	–	3	5
Mizoram	–	–	1
Nagaland	–	–	1
Orissa	5	17	11
Pondicherry	–	–	1
Punjab	–	1	12
Rajasthan	25	8	3
Sikkim	–	–	2
Tamil Nadu	20	14	12
Uttar Pradesh	3	5	3
Uttaranchal	5	7	7
West Bengal	10	16	17
Total	189	181	179

Source: DISE, 2005–2006

construction of schools etc. Explicit subsidies are direct transfer payments to schools and colleges. Such explicit subsidies form a significant proportion of the total education budget. More than one-fifth of the government expenditure on elementary education (primary and upper primary) goes in the form of subsidies to private schools at elementary level. The corresponding proportion is nearly 50 per cent at secondary (including senior secondary) level... Massive subsidies of this kind to private schools are felt to be actually leaving very little for government education institutions. Private schools prosper at the cost of government schools and this phenomenon is described as "private enrichment and public pauperisation"' (Tilak, 2004).

The issue of dual enrolment mentioned earlier (where children are enrolled in government schools to claim entitlements, but actually study in a private school for functional education) also results in considerable wastage. Resources such as teachers, supplies for midday meals and a host of other entitlements are provided on basis of numbers enrolled. This strains the system to its limits and increases the flow of resources into the system, without actually benefiting children in educational terms. Since the phenomenon has not been researched, it is difficult to estimate the degree of wastage involved in this duplication. Nevertheless, this is an impact that the system cannot afford to sustain for long.

Planning for universalisation is rendered incomplete

Mehta (2005) concludes in his study of unrecognised schools in Punjab:

- 'Indicators, such as gross and net enrolment ratios based upon the data collected only from the recognised schools, present only half the picture of universalisation of education.... Unless such data concerning unrecognised schools is also available, a realistic picture of universalisation can never be obtained.

- Planning to enrol all children out of the formal education system will never succeed as many of them are already enrolled in unrecognised schools. Therefore, while developing elementary education plans, enrolment in recognised as well as unrecognised schools should be considered.... Until such time [as this information is available], the planning exercise in its present form will be of limited use and will be treated as an incomplete one.'

Inequity is increased as the system's performance decreases

The growth of the private school system, as mentioned earlier, tends to result in more and more powerful families reducing their dependence on the public system. This, in turn, reduces the accountability that the government school demonstrates, since teachers and officials perceive parents from the most disadvantaged groups as being powerless. The class difference between those in charge of the system (officials, heads, teachers) and the general student population is now almost uniformly wide, leading to less 'sympathy' on the part of service providers. The perception that the government system is now less valued (as the more 'valuable' clients have gone) also acts as a disheartening disincentive. A common reaction observed in recent years might be dubbed 'blaming the victims'; in this case, the community might be held responsible for the poor state of affairs in the government education system. Thus in recent years it has become common to hear teachers and officials blaming parents – for dumping such 'poor stuff' on to them, or not being in a position to fulfil their responsibilities (such as helping children with homework or providing reading material) or being apathetic with regard to ensuring their children's participation in the poor quality education offered to them.

As the most vulnerable groups resort to the government system, teachers and others appear to be thinking of education as a favour – instead of a public service – being provided to the poor and the marginalised. The attitude commonly witnessed is 'having never ever had any access to education, they should be grateful that they are getting at least this!' The fact that education is a service, and the *right* of all children (as enacted by the Indian Parliament in the Right to Education Bill in 2005) tends to get overlooked. In this context, it is worth quoting again the parent interviewed during our case study, who said: 'The quality of teaching or how well teachers teach depends on whose child it is. Teachers pay attention to those who are better off or whose father has some power or if the person is socially known to them. When it comes to our children, they don't bother....'

The notion of education itself is diluted

As the low-fee private schools have marketed themselves to consumers whose ability to assess the education offered is limited (but aspirations of social mobility are not), they have succeeded in creating a 'pop' notion of a good school based on stereotypes. Some of these stereotypes are that a good school is one that has: a building; computers; offers 'English medium'; requires a uniform with a tie, a school bag and a water bottle; maintains 'discipline' through punishment; ensures memorisation; gives plenty of homework; and of course runs regularly. The competition among these schools, as mentioned earlier, is about who *appears* to be better. In this battle of appearances, government schools have emerged the losers to the extent that new efforts at infusing energy or innovation are evaluated by the community in light of the model rampant in the private sector. Thus efforts at banning corporal punishment in government schools or enabling home language use in the classroom are at times *resisted* by the community, on the grounds that this is not what the private schools (or 'good' schools) do.

In an almost unnoticed way, many state governments have decided to 'if you can't beat them, join them'. Many practices of private schools – such as weekly or monthly tests, increased homework or the use of workbooks to promote drill – are being brought into government schools. This is in a context where the National Curriculum Framework (2005) specifically advocates the use of constructivist pedagogy, with which such inputs may not be consistent.

However, the worst impact is that many state school systems have decided to imitate private schools by introducing the teaching of English from grade 1. Policy documents state that this is with a view to 'upgrade' the quality of schools and reduce the migration to private schools. Across the country, distortions are visible as states develop and introduce dated primers to be taught by teachers who themselves have no knowledge of English (beyond perhaps the alphabet). Such time as might have been spent on acquiring basic literacy in the mother tongue or numeracy is now compromised with the effort to learn another language alongside, one that has no reference in spoken form. The difficulties faced by teachers in this near impossible task dishearten them and affect their performance in the teaching of other subjects as well.

In sum, the successful 'selling of the superficial' by the private sector has indeed led to a dilution – both in the notion and practice of education itself.

Options ahead

Private schools are now so much a part of the Indian education sector that wishing them away would be just that – wishful thinking. At the same time, anticipating that a mere extension of existing regulation (which provides government recognition to schools willing to undergo the administrative and commission-giving ordeal involved) would improve quality is equally self-deceptive. A majority of the private schools, both of the elite and subsistence-level educations, find it more expedient to manage without this recognition, rendering the entire system of regulation meaningless. As Mehta (2005) noted, it is more difficult to open a grocery shop than a school.

One difficulty with the parameters used in regulation is that they are all input-related (space, competence of teachers, availability of materials etc.) rather than process-oriented (the *manner* in which the available inputs would be used) or outcome-oriented (the nature and levels of learning that would be attained at the end of given periods). Thus it is possible to have all the required quality parameters and still offer poor education. While the board examinations usually held at the end of grade 5 in many states act as some sort of benchmark, the examinations too, as mentioned earlier, focus on the more limited aspects of learning. Thus even 'teaching to the test' does not lead to high-quality education.

Options

Any discussion on the issue of private- and government-run schools in India rapidly becomes contentious, with the different contenders typically adopting one of the following six positions, each simplistic in its own way:

1. State cannot abdicate its responsibility; a common school system should be brought in to ensure a more equitable access to education;

2. Private schools (since they make use of subsidies) must be compelled to offer free places to children from the poorer sections;

3. Regulate the private school system; keep it on a tight leash to ensure it doesn't exploit the poor;

4. Let the market determine, let consumers (parents) choose. Better still, facilitate aided choice (e.g. through a voucher system);

5. The government system must be improved; or

6. Improve the quality of the private school system; after all what they offer is also very poor.

Each of these positions is also an option in terms of future action. These are discussed below.

The first position clearly defies feasibility, although the Government of Bihar did set up a commission that has submitted a report on the subject. As of the time of writing, the provisions are on paper. Recently attempts have been made (especially in Delhi) to implement the second position, but success as been sporadic and limited. Despite the strength of legislation and a full department to ensure regulation, the flow of the poor into Delhi's more elite schools has been more of a trickle; in the less elite schools, meanwhile, the poor remain absent. Apart from resistance from schools themselves (including in legal form), it is unrealistic to expect that learning spaces will acquire a discrimination-free and classless character that society itself is not able to adopt. Consequently, the poor themselves shy away from the thought of their children being with those from another social class.

The third position is of course what current regulations were supposed to ensure, but have so far failed to achieve over the last several decades.

The fourth option has recently begun to acquire a number of proponents. Prominent among them are Tooley and the Centre for Civil Society. Among those advocating the 'cause' of the private schools, Tooley (2005) is the most forthright:

> 'All of this suggests that if one is interested in serving the needs of the poor in India, then trying to reform the totally inadequate, cumbersome and unaccountable government system is unlikely to be the best way. Instead, reform the regulatory environment to make it suitable for the flourishing of private schools for the poor, help build private voucher schemes using overseas and indigenous philanthropy, and encourage public voucher schemes, so that parents can use their allowance of funding where they see the schools are performing well, rather than wasting them in unresponsive state schools.'

Apart from being founded on the belief that higher test scores is what education is all about, this option also runs the danger of the market not favouring the poor. Aided choice (e.g. through a voucher system) assumes that there are enough suppliers to ensure the competition needed to lead to better quality. While the poorest areas still remain underserved in many ways, the 'pop' notions of school quality referred to earlier might endanger the very idea of education being advocated by the state. (Here there is a conflict between the economists, who hold that however bad it is, education makes a difference for the better, and the educationalists, who consider that bad education is a like a disease no one should want to spread).

The belief that faced with the loss of clientele, government schools would improve, is also naïve. While opening some public services to the private sector has led to some improvement in government operations, this is not the case across the board and tends to work where consumers already pay for the service concerned (e.g. utilities), the day-to-day interface with the consumers is minimal (as in phone services) and the loss of revenue would be high. The functioning of schools is more complex on unit as well as systemic levels. Unlike utilities, classrooms do not function on procedures but principles, which makes the processes (i.e. the service offered) site- or child-specific rather than standardised – thus making it difficult to improve delivery through across–the-board instructions. Hence, there is no guarantee of economic principles 'sorting the problem out'. Having long been seen as a social good, the economic viability of education has never been a critical factor, since it is almost entirely subsidised by the government. In fact, the recent closure of government schools in Kerala due to lack of demand has not had much impact in terms of the desire to improve. Rather, the 'nefarious' practices of the private schools have become the villains, instead of the poor standards of the government schools.

As in the case of private schools, wishing away the government system is hardly an option. In a recent meeting with the Confederation of Indian Industries on Right to Education, the economist Amartya Sen responded to 'a few speakers bemoaning the lack of infrastructure and government's failure'. He made it clear that deficiency in education and health could not be met by the expansion of private schools. Sen was also critical of the voucher system and said, 'Public education is as indispensable as public health care, no matter what supplementary role private schools and private medical care can play' (Press Trust of India, 2007).

Indispensable though the government system is, the option of improving it (number 5, above) is easier said than done. The government's flagship programme, the *Sarva Shiksha Abhiyan*, has now reached a critical point where the last few years have repeatedly shown unacceptably poor levels of learning being attained by children in government schools. A fair number of small and large projects within SSA are underway even now to bring about qualitative improvement. It is the system's inability to recognise and address the increasing diversity of student population (e.g. children who traditionally never attended school – working children, those with a disability, girls from many social groups etc.) that is rendering many efforts futile. Also, a host of governance issues is now more apparent than ever before – corruption, whimsical or thoughtless decision-making, rapid turnover of projects due to inability to wait for results (education is a long gestation activity!), poor implementation and equally poor monitoring. Thus option 5 is being attempted and probably will continue to be attempted for the foreseeable future.

Option 6, improvement in the private school sector, faces a different set of problems. As long as private schools continue to rake in fees, improvement is not on the horizon. Schools 'doing well' often set role models for other aspiring schools, thus reinforcing the 'pop' model of a good school. Any effort to bring about a change ends up having to run counter to this well-established set of 'social inclinations'. In EQUIP (mentioned earlier), considerable engagement with the community was required before qualitative changes were accepted by the paying public as being worth paying for.

One lesson, therefore, is that the focus for improvement has to be as much on the consumer as on the school itself.

The Right to Education Bill

It is in an 'options environment' of this kind that the Right to Education Bill was passed by the Indian parliament in 2005. Some of the above options do find reflection in the Bill. Highlights of the Bill relevant to private schools (Parliamentary Research Service, 2005) are:

- The 86th Constitution Amendment Act added Article 21A affirming that every child between the age of 6 and 14 years has the right to free and compulsory education. The Right to Education Bill seeks to give effect to this Amendment.

- The State shall ensure a school in every child's neighbourhood. Every school shall conform to certain minimum standards defined in the Bill.

- Government schools shall provide free education to all admitted children. Private schools shall admit at least 25 per cent of children from weaker sections; no fee shall be charged to these children. Screening tests at the time of admission and capitation fees are prohibited for all children.

The Bill does not seek to alter the provision of education through the present combination of government schools, aided schools and unaided (private) schools. Some critics have held that adopting the 'common school system' would have been a better option. Others feel that the non-elite private schools, including unrecognised schools, have contributed significantly to the spread of education, and it may even be more cost efficient to encourage these than government schools.

The Bill makes certification from a 'Competent Authority' mandatory before setting up a private school, something that critics feel may lead to corruption and undue interference in school management. Norms (such as teacher-student ratio, physical infrastructure etc.) have been spelt out that would need to be fulfilled by all schools as a pre-requisite for being recognised – and all non-government schools have to be recognised by a Competent Authority or shut down.

At present, the implementation of the Bill is mired in debates and diverse pressures in different directions and it is not clear how the various provisions will be made operational.

Sustained, low-key action towards quality improvement

In the kind of situation described above, there is little scope for radical departures. In a policy-rich nation that is usually found wanting in implementation, even new legislation (such as the Right to Education Bill) does not lend itself easily to improvement efforts. An 'equal and opposite reaction' from society, vested interests and the system itself seeks to co-opt the reform and 'restore' the level to as close to status quo as possible. Such a reaction is also often visible in governance reforms attempted in education, where change has tended to be short-lived before eventually merging in the status that was quo earlier!

So where does this leave those who want to see the most vulnerable groups access the best possible education system? Probably the answer lies in identifying a number of small, doable steps and implementing them over a long period. Three such directions of action are presented below:

1. Mehta (2005) highlights the importance of collecting data from unrecognised schools:

   'Let there be the same set of Data Capture Formats for all schools, i.e. recognised and unrecognised schools. Evidence suggests that even recognised private schools do not happily provide information. They generally suspect that information collected will be used in taking action against them. The unrecognised schools should therefore be given promise of anonymity.... Confidence-building measures over time will help.... convince unrecognised schools.

   'In many states, registration and recognition of private-unaided schools is not mandatory. Therefore, officials have no way of knowing their numbers. The states should widely disseminate provisions for recognition and should make concerted efforts in recognising all eligible unrecognised schools. ... Let states initiate special drives so that all unrecognised schools are registered.'

   Should this step be implemented, schools that today operated 'under the radar' will no longer do so, which in itself might have a salutary impact. This will also make it possible to enable universalisation efforts to be planned in partnership with the private sector and avoid the resource duplication that exists presently, with little outcome to show for it.

2. A useful set of suggestions has emerged from Muralidharan & Kremer (2006):

   - 'Our results have a number of implications. First, efforts to improve the quality of education in India should consider the private as well as public sector – especially since the former are disproportionately located where the public system is failing. For example, policy-makers might consider the possibility of offering short training courses to raise skills among private schoolteachers.

   - Second, the disparities between private and public schools highlight some potential areas for reform in the public sector. The huge salary differential suggests that many public schoolteachers may be receiving enormous rents.

   - Finally, there may be scope for public-private partnerships in education, whether in the form of voucher programmes or otherwise. One issue with voucher programmes is whether there will be an adequate supply response, but the evidence suggests that private schools are already widespread in rural areas and that new schools can be created rapidly.

- There is substantial scope for carefully-designed policy experiments aimed at leveraging the private sector for universal quality education, and it is important to follow these experiments with rigorous evaluation to provide systematic evidence for future policy decisions in this regard.'

3. A set of feasible, less radical measures that have the potential to succeed instead of leading to disruption is described below.

- Since the 'pop' notion of a school is emerging as the de facto standard in operation, 'consumer education' would help in 'counter marketing'. Perhaps one critical step that may be taken relatively easily is to frame process and outcome parameters to ascertain and attain quality for *all* schools, government, aided or unaided private schools, without offering the choice to evade being assessed against such parameters. In this, it is not standardisation but standards-orientation that is sought, with scope for context-based implementation.

Once framed, such standards should be widely publicised to let people know about what to expect and what is the minimum they should get for their money/effort in a private **or** government school. The intention would be to generate a clear demand and public insistence on qualitative processes and real learning outcomes (as opposed to mere marks). One recent (contextual) standards-development effort of the Government of India entitled Advancement of Educational Performance Through Teacher Support (ADEPTS), initiated with the UN Children's Fund (UNICEF) support, involved the development of *performance* benchmarks for teachers and teacher-support institutions, at the district and sub-district levels (Shukla, 2007). The willingness shown by many states to 'roll out' such standards is an encouraging sign that the system may eventually orient itself to function in a more standards-oriented manner.

- An accompanying requirement would be to build the capacity at various levels to attain these standards. Teachers, managers and state/district-level institutions would need a range of inputs spread over a long term. *At present the institutional capability and strength needed to effect such capacity development remains the single greatest weakness of the Indian system.* Investment by the government and support from external funding should be welcome in this regard.

- Finally, the assessment of quality might work best were it in the hands of those who have a real stake in children's education – parents and communities. There is a need to empower as well as build the capacity of local bodies to assess quality of education through a massive programme. Such community-based monitoring could provide the system real-time information on the status of schools, which could then use its resources to bring about improvement rather than supervision.

Idealistic though it might seem, in a democratic polity it is by reducing rather than increasing control that such improvement may be brought about. Naturally, this would need to be backed by efforts to capacitate all involved. Given the massive scale of the system and the nature of educational enterprise, perhaps the way forward is to enable a transfer of *concern*, rather than just a set of *instructions*. This generation of ownership and capacity at various levels might lead the multiple stakeholders to ask appropriate questions and enable them to work towards answers most suited to their context.

Notes

1. £1 was equivalent to Rs.78.76 as of January 2008.
2. The District Information System for Education (DISE, described in the next chapter) was introduced as the national EMIS, a database on all key education variables related to access, participation, teachers, facilities and infrastructure. In 2003, DISE was extended to the entire country as the official data reporting system for elementary education.
3. At the time of the survey, the rupee was valued at around Rs.45 = $1. The minimum wage fixed by the government was around Rs.100.

5

NIGERIA

Dr Abdurrahman Umar

Introduction: definitions and conceptualisations

In Nigeria, schools are generally categorised as either government or private schools. From interaction with officials of the federal and state ministries of education, local government education secretaries and proprietors of private schools during field-work in the sampled states, the defining characteristics of private schools are:

- Ownership – owned by an individual, a religious or community organisation etc. and not by government;

- Source of funding – fees, no matter how small, are paid by parents/guardians, even if some form of financial support or a high-level of financial support is provided by government, an individual philanthropist, a corporate body etc.

- Type of management – such a school is privately managed and therefore not among the schools managed by the federal or state ministry of education or the Local Government Education Authority (LGEA).

The Nigerian Education Management Information System (NEMIS) and the State Education Management Information System (SEMIS) (in those states that have it) categorise schools simply into the two categories: government or private, as above. This means all schools that are not owned and managed by government are grouped together and referred to as private schools. This includes those that receive substantial financial and material support from government (e.g. Qur'anic and Islamiyya schools in states such as Kano and Sokoto), even though there are very significant differences among them in terms of goals, type and amount of fees charged, curricula and management systems etc. Private schools can be subdivided into those that are registered with and recognised by government and have met the prescribed minimum standards for the establishment of schools; and those that have not registered or have failed to meet the minimum standards and are therefore not recognised by government. It should be noted that the general neglect and collapse of public schools in the late 1980s and 1990s has led to a dramatic increase in the number of private schools, particularly of the unregistered and unrecognised variety. It is widely believed that there are more unregistered private schools than the registered schools captured in official statistics, which include NEMIS and SEMIS.

Private schooling in Nigeria: a review of relevant literature

The neglect and collapse of public primary schools in Nigeria in the 1980s and 1990s has not yet been fully addressed in most states and has brought about the deterioration of the quality of tuition in these schools. This in turn has led to a significant expansion of private primary schools, as more and more parents seek an alternative to public schools.

Despite the steady increase in the number of private primary schools and the significant proportion of children enrolled in them, they have not received the attention of researchers. Private schooling in Nigeria is seriously understudied and very few studies exist on the number, location, operational modalities and the quality of tuition private schools provide. However, concerns about Nigeria's ability to meet the goal of Education for All (EFA) and the Millennium Development Goals (MDGs) have led to a renewed interest in private schools and the extent to which they have provided access to basic education.

One of the most serious gaps in the literature on private education is lack of reliable data on the number and distribution of private primary and secondary schools in Nigeria, including data on teachers, teaching-learning facilities, enrolment and the socio-economic background of pupils who are enrolled in such schools. In an attempt to address this gap, *Basic and Senior Secondary Education Statistics in Nigeria: 2004 and 2005* was published by the Federal Ministry of Education in 2006. This publication provides data on not only public primary and secondary schools, but also pre-primary and private schools, learners with special needs and unenrolled children. It also includes NEMIS data and thematic mapping of indicators to the local government authority (LGA) level.[1] This publication remains the most current and easily accessible source of data on private schools in Nigeria and it covers more private schools than any previous publication. However, its coverage of private schools is not comprehensive. The report itself admits that 'there still appears to be many private schools (registered and unregistered) that are not captured in the system.'[2]

The near-total collapse of public primary schools and the deterioration in the quality of tuition they provide has led to the steady expansion of private schools. That in turn has engendered scholarly interest in private education and its contributions to EFA. Such studies include Tooley (2005a, 2006), Tooley and Dixon (2006) and Adelabu and Rose (2004).

Tooley (2005a) conducted a study of private schools in Lagos (Nigeria), Ghana, Kenya and India. He conducted a systematic census and survey of all public and private primary and secondary schools in selected low-income areas and tested 160 sampled schools in Lagos in mathematics, English and social studies.

The major findings of the study were that 'the majority of poor parents choose private-unaided schools for their children', and that 'in Lagos state, an estimated 75 per cent of school children are in private schools, with a larger proportion (33 per cent compared to 25 per cent) in unregistered private than in government schools'.[3] Tooley also found that the private schools did better in English and mathematics tests than government schools and cost significantly less in terms of teacher costs. The study also revealed school enrolment in private schools to be grossly underestimated, mainly because government statistics exclude unregistered/unrecognised private schools. Pupil-teacher ratios in unrecognised/unregistered private schools were found to be 'usually about half those in government schools... and there was a significantly higher level of teaching going on in private-unaided schools than in government schools.'[4] The study's major implication is that private schools have an important role to play in helping government to attain EFA targets.

In a follow up study, entitled '"De facto" privatisation of education and the poor: implications of a study from sub-Saharan Africa and India', Tooley and Dixon (2006) used the findings of Tooley (2005a) to examine the concept of de facto privatisation. This they defined as a situation 'in which responsibilities for education have been transferred de facto to the private sector, through the rapid growth of private schools rather than de jure, through reform or legislation.'[5] The focus of the study was also Lagos (Nigeria), Hyderabad (India), Ga (Ghana) and Nairobi (Kenya). They attributed the growth of de facto privatisation to poor quality of government schools, lack of accountability in public schools (teachers in private schools are more accountable) and the fact that the number of public schools is inadequate vis-à-vis the social demand for primary education. They identified from the literature on private education, three reasons why private schools for the poor are not seen as important tools for the attainment of the Millennium Development Goals in education and subjected them to scrutiny and further investigation in the light of studies conducted in Lagos, Ga and Hyderabad. These three reasons were:

- 'Private schools are inequitable because they charge fees, thus making them out of reach of the poorest of the poor'; and they 'exacerbate' gender inequalities 'as parents prefer to send their boys to them';

- The quality of tuition in private schools is poor, thus making them more accessible to the poor is not a desirable thing to do; and

- Private schools can undermine the public school system 'if poor parents support private education.'[6]

The findings of the follow-up study revealed that:

- More pupils were enrolled in private schools than in public schools. In Lagos state, 'two-thirds of primary school enrolment was in private schools and that enrolment in unregistered or unrecognised private schools exceeded that in government schools';

- In terms of gender enrolment, 'schools reported 50 per cent of girls and boys... (thus) private schools were no different from government schools in gender enrolment';

- Teacher commitment was greater and the rate of absenteeism lower in private schools;

- Private schools out-performed government schools in achievement tests in English and mathematics. In Lagos state, 'the mean maths score advantage over government schools was about 14 and 19 percentage points respectively in private registered and unregistered schools, while in English it was 22 and 29 percentage points'[7]; and

- There is no evidence to suggest that an increased role for private schools in the attainment of EFA would inevitably undermine public schooling.

These findings were further examined in Tooley (2006) with a view to identifying the specific ways in which the quality and effectiveness of private schools for the poor may be improved through the intervention of international donor agencies. These include helping private school proprietors to improve their infrastructure through microfinance loans, investment in educational technology and 'assisting the market in the creation of educational brand names that will help parents make their judgements in a more informed way.'[8]

However, although the studies reviewed above deal with the potentials for private education to contribute to the attainment of EFA, they should be treated with caution. In the Nigerian context, they focused on only one subset of private schools, i.e. those that are privately managed and privately funded and receive no state funds at all. In some parts of Nigeria, such as Kano state, private Islamiyya schools enrol more children than all other types of schools put together. In Kano state there are currently 3 million children enrolled in 28,000 Islamiyya and Qur'anic schools, as compared with nearly 4,000 public and private schools catering for over 1.5 million children.[9] Similarly, the studies focused on only one state in Nigeria, i.e. Lagos state. This raises questions about the extent to which the findings can be generalised to other states in the country given the diversity and complexity of Nigeria.

In a study of non-state provision of basic education in Ekiti, Borno, Enugu, Oyo, Benue and Kano states of Nigeria, Adelabu and Rose (2004) critically discussed the historical evolution and current status of private schooling in Nigeria, using secondary and case study data generated from several states. The study indicates that:

- the expansion of private schooling was largely due to 'state failure to provide primary schooling which is both accessible and of appropriate quality.' Although there is no data on the growth of private sector education over a long period of time, some of the current evidence indicates, 'private primary schools comprise as much as one-fifth of the total number of schools in some states'.[10]

- Unrecognised/unregistered schools do provide access to a significant number of children, particularly in urban and peri-urban areas. Although '...in some cases they appear to be offering a better quality of education compared with some government schools, this is still below a desirable level.'

- Unapproved schools will continue to exist and it is therefore desirable to take measures that would bring them under greater state control so as to enforce standards, given the legitimate concerns that... 'some unapproved schools are taking advantage of the gap in the market, and are more concerned with making money than the quality of education provided.'[11]

The study emphasised the need for further research on the size of the private sector, '... the relationships between different types of schools (government, approved, unapproved) in terms of access and quality, including reasons for parental choice of different types of schools.... and how different aspects of standards influence parental decisions over the types of schools to send their children to.' Other areas for further research suggested by the study include the roles being played by Islamiyya schools in northern Nigeria in providing access to education and how they can be integrated into the formal system, and the impact of the proposed return of mission schools (which were taken over by the state in the 1970s) on access to schooling for children from poor households.[12]

Research methodology and data analysis

The major concern of this study was to investigate the 'impact of low-cost private sector education on achieving Universal Primary Education (UPE) in Nigeria.' It sought to determine the extent to which low-cost private schooling has contributed to access to UPE in Nigeria. Its fundamental assumption is that despite the phenomenal expansion of the public primary sector, it has not been able to adequately meet the social demand for primary education. At the same time, the recent collapse of the sector in terms of quality of tuition has prompted many poor parents to seek alternatives in low-cost private schools, which in their view are qualitatively better than public primary schools. Thus this study addresses three key issues:

1. From the demand side, are parents in the low-income groups (in this case peasants, the working class and the lower-middle class) sending a significant proportion of their children to low-cost private schools, in spite of the existence and accessibility to public primary schools? A related question is the extent to which low-cost private schools have expanded to meet the social demand for primary education, and the presumed better quality of the tuition provided in such schools given the widely acknowledged deterioration of quality in the public sector?

2. How do the low-cost private schools compare with the public schools in terms of quality of tuition and are the poor who prefer low-cost private education getting 'value for money' as measured by pupils' performance in public examinations or other measures of pupils' learning outcomes – for example, the periodic monitoring of learning achievement conducted by the Federal Ministry of Education?

3. What is the future of low-cost private schools? Will they continue to grow in the light of the general dissatisfaction with the quality of public primary schools or

would they shrink and or stabilise at their current levels as government takes measures to enhance the quality of tuition of public schools through the provision of improved learning environments, text books, more qualified teachers, strengthening of the inspectorate etc?

In order to address these issues, data were gathered to answer the following research questions:

- How many low-cost private schools are there? Are there certain areas where they are concentrated, e.g. urban versus rural; or in states/districts with poor-quality government schools?

- Are there any size patterns? Are low-cost private schools smaller or larger than the average government schools in their areas?

- What is the enrolment? What is the percentage of students in such schools as compared with other types of schools, including other non-state schools? Is the gender balance different from government schools?

- What are the staffing patterns? How do pupil-teacher ratios (PTRs) and teacher qualifications compare with the state sector?

- What are the fees? How do these vary between clusters of private schools? How do costs compare with government schools when one includes other parental costs such as uniforms, pens, exercise books etc?

- What is the quality of low-cost private primary schools as compared with that of public schools? Are children in low-cost private schools getting 'value for money' as compared with their counterparts in the public sector?

The research methodology used in this study is inter-method triangulation and the methods triangulated are:

1. A critical review of the secondary data on private schooling. These include published and unpublished studies on private schooling, government reports, EMIS etc;

2. Primary (case study) data obtained through:

    - Key informant interviewing; the key informants interviewed were policy-makers at the state, local and federal levels, proprietors of private schools, the Nigeria Union of Teachers (NUT), Parent Teacher Associations (PTAs), the Association of Private School Owners at the state and local levels, school inspectors and community leaders; and

    - Focus group discussions with teachers, pupils, head teachers and proprietors of private and public schools selected for this study.

The data analysis: national secondary data

Number and distribution of private primary schools, classrooms and enrolment by state

According to the data published by the Federal Ministry of Education in 2006, in 2005 there were 9,318 private primary schools in Nigeria, with a total enrolment of 1,578,635 pupils (814,693 male, 763,942 female) and 105,326 teachers and 61,223 classrooms. Enrolment increased from 4.6 per cent in 1998 to 7.25 per cent in 2005.

As table 5.1 below shows, all the 36 states and the Federal Capital Territory (FCT) have a significant number of private primary schools. Lagos state has the highest number of schools at 1,251, followed by Oyo state (879 schools), Ogun state (561 schools),[13] Delta state (462 schools) and Kano state (382 schools). The state with the fewest private primary schools is Zamfara (24 schools) and the FCT Abuja (3).[14]

In 2005, there were 22,267,407 pupils enrolled in primary schools. Of these, 20,688,772 pupils were enrolled in public schools, while 1,578,635 were enrolled in private schools.[15] Table 5.2, below, provides comparative data of public and private schools in terms of enrolment, number of teachers, pupil-teacher ratio (PTR), pupil-qualified-teacher ratio (PQTR) and gender gap.

Table 5.3 shows that enrolment in private primary schools constitutes only 7 per cent of total enrolment. However, it should be noted that this figure is only for registered/recognised private schools and excludes unregistered/unrecognised schools. The figure will increase significantly if the latter are added to the total. Private schools tend to do better in terms of PTR, which is 15.07 as compared with 41.86 for public schools; PQTR which is 38.21 as compared with 80.42 for public schools; and pupil-classroom ratio which is 20.00 for private schools as against 91.25 for public schools (see Table 5.2). However private schools had a higher withdrawal rate of 2.02 per cent as compared with 0.88 for public schools (see Table 5.3), and a pupil-to-core-textbook ratio of 5.59 as compared with 3.10 for public schools.

Quality of private and public schools

The quality of schools has at least two dimensions. First, the quality of inputs such as teachers and teaching-learning facilities etc. and secondly the performance of pupils in external examinations and assessments and the performance of school graduates. Ideally, it should be possible to compare the quality of public and private schools along these dimensions. However, while comparative data exist for inputs such as teachers and classrooms, there is no readily available comparative data on teaching-learning facilities, toilets, playgrounds etc. or on performance in public examinations. The only source of comparative data on academic performance of pupils in public and private schools is the Monitoring of Learning Achievement (MLA) report of 2003, which compares the learning achievement of primary grade 4 and 6 pupils in literacy, numeracy and life skills, and which was published in 2005.[16]

Table 5.1 Number of private primary schools, classrooms, enrolment and teachers (2005)

S/N	State	No. of Schools	No. of Class-rooms	Enrolment primary				Teachers					PTR	PCR
				M	F	Total (M+F)	%F Enrol	M	F	Total (M+F)	%F Teach			
1	Abia	199	1,569	20,245	19,859	40,104	49.52	395	2,276	2,671	85.21	19.77	33.87
2	Adamawa	122	594	11,740	10,902	22,642	48.15	751	608	1,359	44.74	20.37	47.54
3	Akwa Ibom	225	2,059	24,895	25,138	50,033	50.24	953	2,276	3,229	70.49	21.89	34.04
4	Anambra	230	1,812	23,053	22,004	45,057	48.84	239	2,743	2,982	91.99	15.51	25.69
5	Bauchi	115	597	25,017	19,735	44,752	44.10	881	576	1,457	39.53	34.14	87.18
6	Bayelsa	54	313	4,094	3,940	8,034	49.04	233	355	588	60.37	19.28	35.20
7	Benue	247	893	26,955	23,558	50,513	46.64	1,403	666	2,069	32.19	26.92	65.40
8	Borno	172	859	21,637	17,449	39,086	44.64	1,023	689	1,712	40.25	21.14	44.12
9	Cross River	173	1,216	11,677	11,650	23,327	49.94	673	1,362	2,035	66.93	18.05	30.48
10	Delta	462	3,535	34,600	33,187	67,787	48.96	1,508	3,899	5,407	72.11	16.48	25.32
11	Ebonyi	77	392	9,873	9,973	19,846	50.25	195	542	737	73.54	30.45	58.61
12	Edo	293	1,636	25,203	23,593	48,796	48.35	972	2,260	3,232	69.93	19.31	37.33
13	Ekiti	152	861	7,480	7,132	14,612	48.81	471	1,103	1,574	70.08	9.77	17.51
14	Enugu	50	396	5,583	5,201	10,784	48.23	107	536	643	83.36	18.87	32.39
15	FCT	3	14	62	38	100	38.00	-	6	6	100.00	51.00	21.86
16	Gombe	206	697	19,952	21,338	41,290	51.68	845	508	1,353	37.55	30.18	57.51
17	Imo	233	1,445	24,966	23,617	48,583	48.61	504	1,908	2,412	79.10	23.97	39.69
18	Jigawa	52	165	6,506	6,252	12,758	49.00	250	78	328	23.78	35.72	78.82
19	Kaduna	373	2,238	38,920	37,120	76,040	48.82	1,952	2,315	4,267	54.25	20.30	39.96

S/N	State	No. of Schools	No. of Class-rooms	Enrolment primary				Teachers				PTR	PCR
				M	F	Total (M+F)	%F Enrol	M	F	Total (M+F)	%F Teach		
20	Kano	382	1,589	49,767	53,254	103,021	51.69	2,232	1,593	3,825	41.65	24.34	61.22
21	Katsina	80	274	8,726	6,238	14,964	41.69	467	339	806	42.06	21.68	62.02
22	Kebbi	67	256	8,119	6,518	14,637	44.53	362	272	634	42.90	24.17	67.61
23	Kogi	221	1,263	24,259	23,925	48,184	49.65	880	1,320	2,200	60.00	24.84	44.63
24	Kwara	350	2,316	27,227	24,159	51,386	47.01	1,116	2,195	3,311	66.29	17.59	25.00
25	Lagos	1,251	13,510	87,271	85,827	173,098	49.58	5,000	13,379	18,379	72.80	11.95	16.34
26	Nasarawa	153	785	13,455	11,960	25,415	47.06	710	691	1,401	49.32	21.90	42.84
27	Niger	342	1,598	29,391	24,565	53,956	45.53	1,696	1,724	3,420	50.41	18.25	39.40
28	Ogun	561	3,987	37,573	36,200	73,773	49.07	2,070	4,791	6,861	69.83	12.67	22.31
29	Ondo	500	2,453	35,155	34,103	69,258	49.24	1,822	3,591	5,413	66.34	13.14	28.38
30	Osun	480	2,518	20,237	19,329	39,566	48.85	1,245	3,004	4,249	70.70	11.24	19.43
31	Oyo	879	5,557	58,156	56,874	115,030	49.44	3,254	7,626	10,880	70.09	13.02	25.96
32	Plateau	217	1,597	16,756	15,666	32,422	48.32	919	1,138	2,057	55.32	22.40	28.34
33	Rivers	97	1,018	9,098	9,350	18,448	50.68	231	835	1,066	78.33	22.08	24.55
34	Sokoto	114	356	24,714	15,825	40,539	39.04	539	276	815	33.87	50.39	113.77
35	Taraba	130	540	13,234	11,696	24,930	46.92	789	490	1,279	38.31	20.95	49.24
36	Yobe	32	158	5,275	4,183	9,458	44.23	205	152	357	42.58	28.69	66.74
37	Zamfara	24	157	3,822	2,584	6,406	40.34	168	144	312	46.15	24.18	50.63
Total		9,318	61,223	814,693	763,942	1,578,635	48.39	37,060	68,266	105,326	64.81	22.61	43.27

Table 5.2 Primary education indicators for Nigeria (2005)

Indicator	Public	Private	Total	Demographic data	Female	Male	All
Gender parity index (GPI)	0.83	0.97	0.84	Pop. aged 6-11 yrs	11,394,046	11,806,402	23,200,448
Gender Ratio (Net)	0.85	0.95	0.85	Pop. aged 6 yrs	2,043,969	2,115,536	4,159,505
Gender gap (Gross) in %			16.24	Not enrolled, aged 6-11 yrs	2,602,795	1,048,539	3,631,334
Gender gap (Net) in %			8.59	ASER aged 6-11 yrs	77.85	91.83	84.97
Gender gap – teachers in %	4.40	-30.09	-1.63	Gross (apparent) intake rate	99.24	116.11	107.82
No. of schools reported	50,742	9.019	59,761	Net intake rate primary 1	61.49	72.42	67.04
Pupil-teacher ratio (PTR)	41.86	15.07	37.18	Gross enrolment ratio	87.72	103.95	95.98
Pupil-qualified-teacher ratio (PQTR)	80.42	38.21	74.58	CASER	50.08	58.67	54.45
Pupil-classroom ratio	91.25	20.00	72.85	Net enrolment rate	77.16	91.12	84.26
Teacher-to-classroom ratio	2.18	1.33	1.96	Transition rate into JS1	53.72	47.21	50.08
Pupil-to-core-textbook ratio	3.10	5.59	3.21	School completion rate	70.21	84.95	77.71
				School survival	69.54	67.31	68.28

Table 5.3 Enrolment data for Nigeria (2005)

	All schools			Public schools			Private schools		
	Female	Male	Total	Female	Male	Total	Female	Male	Total
Enrolment (primary 1-6)	9,994,361	12,273,046	22,267,407	9,230,419	11,458,39	20,688,72	763,942	814,693	1,578,635
Enrolment in primary 1	2,028,449	2,456,323	4,484,772	1,866,985	2,284,481	4,151,466	161,464	171,842	333,306
Enrolment in primary 6	1,237,547	1,553,239	2,790,786	1,169,132	1,477,164	2,646,296	68,415	76,075	144,490
Repetition rate	0.03	0.03	0.03	0.03	0.03	0.03	0.02	0.02	0.02
% Repeaters	2.98	2.77	2.87	3.09	2.84	2.95	1.70	1.86	1.78
% Withdrawals	1.10	0.95	1.02	1.02	0.88	0.94	2.05	1.99	2.02
Number of teachers	304,382	294,599	598,981	236,267	257,992	494,259	68,115	36,607	104,722
No. of qualified teachers	184,122	114,451	298,573	155,923	101,339	257,262	28,199	13,112	41,311
% qualified teachers	60.49	38.85	49.85	65.99	39.28	52.05	41.40	35.82	39.45
Teachers: non-teaching ratio	11.51	6.72	8.52	20.31	7.09	10.29	4.60	4.90	4.70

Table 5.4 below shows the distribution of scores in numeracy tests (grade 4, also called primary 4) by state and school type.[17] The table shows that:

- Pupils' performance is generally unsatisfactory;

- The mean score for private schools is 37 per cent as compared with 33.34 per cent for public schools. Thus the pupils in private schools outperformed the national mean score of 33.74[18]; and

- The pupils in private schools in 25 states and the FCT performed better than pupils in public schools: mean scores of private schools are higher (37.0) than that of public schools (33.34).

Table 5.4 Distribution of scores in numeracy tests by state and school type

S/N	State	Public			Private		
		N	Mean %	SD	N	Mean %	SD
1	Abia	661	26.03	14.40	91	39.21	15.08
2	Adamawa	502	21.30	15.80	145	28.73	18.94
3	Akwa-Ibom	596	28.13	13.64	15	35.47	9.30
4	Anambra	705	31.47	17.65	36	22.61	9.38
5	Bauchi	563	44.91	22.81	34	55.24	10.99
6	Bayelsa	360	23.54	13.40	31	13.48	4.70
7	Benue	768	40.80	21.95	-	-	-
8	Borno	368	21.46	14.68	87	10.28	8.40
9	Cross River	120	34.40	13.28	-	-	-
10	Delta	369	26.48	15.20	75	50.03	18.87
11	Ebonyi	658	20.22	11.35	-	-	-
12	Edo	520	33.64	20.54	-	-	-
13	Ekiti	749	36.01	15.61	31	26.71	6.74
14	Enugu	262	49.97	21.29	74	44.65	29.62
15	Gombe	614	35.25	24.84	53	53.58	30.06
16	Imo	377	25.59	12.43	262	27.37	15.41
17	Jigawa	688	45.11	23.01	22	85.09	5.75
18	Kaduna	436	51.02	23.64	130	36.66	17.70
19	Kano	535	34.40	21.22	60	55.33	12.56
20	Katsina	539	28.32	22.81	61	43.84	18.90
21	Kebbi	559	41.65	24.30	30	37.33	7.49
22	Kogi	520	31.10	18.43	153	35.91	14.49
23	Kwara	539	32.48	16.55	60	33.65	9.63
24	Lagos	726	31.65	14.37	63	42.67	18.06
25	Nasarawa	621	23.66	16.91	120	34.38	22.75
26	Niger	536	28.85	18.31	214	42.14	17.00
27	Ogun	394	46.68	19.96	61	66.00	23.40
28	Ondo	627	34.98	13.96	107	35.55	14.43
29	Osun	513	31.60	15.85	83	37.57	11.93
30	Oyo	774	36.11	19.28	42	42.43	13.62
31	Plateau	542	29.24	17.54	199	28.79	12.83
32	Sokoto	710	26.11	17.51	89	41.01	12.93
33	Taraba	532	45.76	21.45	68	40.41	14.85
34	Yobe	693	39.29	21.07	30	39.00	9.95
35	Zamfara	780	33.19	23.77	-	-	-
36	FCT	76	23.58	12.89	15	52.40	17.01
37	National	19,514	33.34	20.34	2546	37.00	19.93

The results of the tests on literacy and life skills also indicate a similar pattern, with private schools outperforming their counterparts in public schools. The mean literacy scores are 33.96 per cent for public schools and 46.65 per cent for private schools. The private schools performed better than the national mean score of 35.05 per cent. Similarly, the mean score of pupils from private schools was 53.28 per cent in life skills; this was better than that of the public schools, which was 42.77. Furthermore, the private school mean score was higher than the national mean score of 43.81 per cent.

The corresponding mean scores for primary 6 (class or grade 6) pupils are given below in Table 5.5.

Thus, in all the three areas tested during the MLA project, private schools did better than their public school counterparts. This is consistent with the findings of other studies, notably Tooley's (2005a) study of private schools in Lagos, cited above. What can account for that? There are many reasons, some of which include: teachers in private schools tend to demonstrate higher levels of commitment and lower levels of absenteeism than their counterparts in public schools; and there is a higher level of teacher accountability and closer supervision of teachers in private schools as compared with public schools.

Private schooling in Nigeria: summary of the national context

Based on the above discussion and analysis, the current situation of private schools in Nigeria is summarised below.

• Private schools are those schools that are not owned or managed by government and charge fees for the tuition they provide, even if they also receive substantial financial support from government. Private schools can be categorised into those which have met the minimum standards set by government for the establishment of schools and are therefore registered and recognised by government, and those which do not meet the minimum standards or did not seek registration and are therefore unregistered and unrecognised by government.

• The most serious gap in the literature on private education is the lack of reliable data on the number and distribution of private primary and secondary schools in Nigeria, including data on teachers, teaching-learning facilities, enrolment, the

Table 5.5 Distribution of test scores for primary 6 pupils by school type [19]

S/No.	Subject area	National mean %	Mean public schools	Mean private schools
1	Numeracy test	35.73	35.09	40.35
2	Literacy test	41.53	41.22	48.17
3	Life skills	25.42	25.40	25.65

socio-economic background of pupils/students who are enrolled in such schools etc.

• There are more unregistered/unrecognised private schools than registered/recognised private schools. Unregistered/unrecognised private schools are not included in official statistics. There is therefore gross under-counting of private schools and the number of children enrolled in them.

• The collapse of public primary schools has led to a steady increase in the number of private schools. Recent data indicate that enrolment in private schools increased from 4.6 per cent in 1998 to 7.25 in 2005. Lagos state has the highest number of private schools (1,251), followed by Oyo state (879), Ogun state (561), Delta state (462) and Kano state (382). The areas with the fewest private primary schools are Zamfara state (24 schools) and the FCT Abuja (3).

• Even if public schools are rehabilitated and the quality of the tuition they provide improves, private-sector education will still continue to grow and remain relevant. This is mainly because the number of public schools is insufficient to meet the social demand for primary education, particularly in poor urban centres; the vast majority of such schools currently operate a shift system in order to accommodate the increase in enrolment. In addition, many parents will for various reasons still continue to patronise private primary schools and will prefer them to public schools. The growth of integrated Islamiyya schools in many parts of northern Nigeria, such as Kano, may be partly explained in terms of not only their perceived quality, but the fact that Islamic religious knowledge is central to their curricula, in addition to secular subjects such as science, English, mathematics and social studies etc.

• As at 2005, there were 9,318 private primary schools in Nigeria with a total enrolment of 1,578,635 pupils (814,693 male, 763,942 female) and 105,326 teachers and 61,223 classrooms.

• As at 2005, there were 22,267,407 pupils enrolled in primary schools. Of these, 20,688,772 pupils were enrolled in public schools, while 1,578,635 were enrolled in private schools. Thus enrolment in private primary schools constitutes only 7.08 per cent of total enrolment. However, it should be noted that this figure is only for registered/recognised private schools and excludes unregistered/unrecognised schools.

• Private schools tend to do better in terms of PTR, which is 15.07 as compared with 41.86 for public schools. PQTR is 38.21 in private schools as compared with 80.42 for public schools, and the pupil-classroom ratio is 20.00 for private schools as against 91.25 for public schools.

• The only source of comparative data on academic performance of pupils in public and private schools is the Monitoring of Learning Achievement (MLA) report of 2003, which compares the learning achievement of primary 4 and primary 6 pupils in literacy, numeracy and life skills and was published in 2005.[20] The report of the MLA study indicates that in all the three areas tested during the MLA project, private schools did better than their public school counterparts. Some of the reasons for the differences in performance between public and private schools include: the fact that teachers in private schools tend to demonstrate higher levels of commitment and lower levels of absenteeism than their counterparts in public schools; and there is a higher level of teacher accountability and closer supervision of teachers in private schools as compared with public schools.

• There are no comprehensive reliable national data on the growth of private schools over a long period of time; however, some of the existing evidence suggests that in some states, up to one-fifth of schools are private.

Analysis of case study data

The three states sampled for this study are Imo in south-eastern Nigeria, Kaduna in the north and Ogun in the south-west. Table 5.6 summarises the statistical data available for the three states.[21]

As can be seen from Table 5.6 of the three states, Ogun has the highest number of teachers employed and the highest number of private schools. Private schools in Ogun also have the smallest pupil-classroom ratio and the lowest pupil-teacher ratio. Kaduna state, however, has the lowest pupil-qualified-teacher ratio at 1:20 in private schools. Although Ogun state has the highest rate for pupils transitioning to junior secondary school (JSS), Imo has by far the highest school completion rate. There are 12 per cent more boys enrolled in primary school across the three states. Kaduna makes up the vast majority of this discrepancy as over 114,000 more boys than girls are enrolled in school in this state.

Case study data generated from public and private schools in urban and rural local government areas is set out in Table 5.7. It shows that the total enrolment in the private schools sampled for this study was 3,746 made up of 1,799 boys and 1,947 girls, while the total enrolment in public primary schools was 10,190 made up of 5,027 boys and 5,163 girls. Total enrolments in private schools therefore make up 26.9 per cent of total public and private enrolments in the selected schools. In the selected private schools in Kaduna and Ogun there are slightly more boys than girls enrolled, whereas in Imo there are 238 more girls than boys.

How do the two types of school compare in terms of number of teachers, qualifications of teachers, availability and adequacy of classrooms etc? Table 5.9 provides data on the number and qualification of teachers in the selected private and public schools.

The public and private schools selected and their pupil enrolments are given in Table 5.8.

Table 5.6 Available statistical data on schools in Imo, Kaduna and Ogun states

	Imo				Kaduna				Ogun				Total three states
	Public	Private	Private as proportion of total	Total	Public	Private	Private as proportion of total	Total	Public	Private	Private as proportion of total	Total	Total
Number of primary schools	1,205	233	16.2%	1,438	6,759	373	5.2%	7,132	1,312	558	29.8%	1,870	10,440
Number of teachers	15,179	2,412	13.7%	17,591	25,426	4,267	14.4%	29,729	15,977	6,889	30.1%	22,866	70,186
Male	307,375	29,966	8.9%	337,341	485,769	38,920	7.4%	524,689				164,746	1,026,776
Female	310,647	23,617	7.1%	334,264	373,446	37,120	9.0%	410,566				158,454	903,284
Gross enrolment rate				101.01				84.59				84.75	
Male				102.39									
Female				99.66									
Male				97.46									
Female				94.94									
Transition rate into junior secondary school (JSS)				25.42				43.28				80.24	
Male				22.08									
Female				29.51									
School completion rate (SCR)				106.34				50.14				67.75	
Male				107.94				57.51					
Female				104.75				42.34					
Pupil-teacher ratio (PTR)	1:40.78	1:20.99		1:38.18	1:36.7	1:17.8		1:31.5	1:23.27	1:10.71			
Pupil-qualified-teacher ratio (PQTR)	1:53.51	1:68.91		1:54.39		1:20.3		1:61.2	1:30.71	1:26.52			

Table 5.7 Urban versus rural local government areas (LGAs) in the three states

	Imo	*Kaduna*	*Ogun*
Urban LGA	Owerri Municipal	Kaduna North	Abeokuta South
Rural LGA	Aboh Mbaise	Igabi	Water side
	Okigwe	Chikun	Odogbolu

Table 5.9 shows that the total number of teachers in the selected private schools was 234, of whom 165 (70.5 per cent) had the Nigerian Certificate of Education (NCE – the prescribed minimum teaching qualification) or above. There were 502 teachers in the public schools, of whom 376 (74.9 per cent) possessed the NCE or above. Based on the enrolment figures given in Table 5.8 – 10,190 pupils in public schools and 3,746 in private schools – the average PTR for the selected public schools was 1:20.3, and 1:16.0 for private schools. The pupil-to-qualified-teacher ratio for public schools was 1:27.1, while that of the private schools was 1:22.7. Overall, therefore, private schools had lower and better PTR and PQTR than their public school counterparts. Kaduna state, which has the highest population of public school pupils, also has the highest PQTR and this impacts upon the public school average PQTR.

In terms of the adequacy of facilities (classrooms, toilets, playground, library, computers etc.) all the public schools sampled for this study in Imo state reported that these were inadequate to meet the needs of their enrolled students. Five of the six selected private schools reported that their classrooms to be inadequate; four out of six of them reported that they had adequate textbooks; only two out of six of them reported having adequate toilets; and three of them said they had an adequate playground, library and computers.

In Ogun, the private schools are also ahead of their public counterparts in terms of facilities. The classrooms in three out of the six public schools are not in good shape and require repair or renovation. However, in terms of availability of outdoor space, the public schools had adequate playgrounds compared with their private school counterparts. In fact, two of the six private schools selected did not have a playground at all.

In Kaduna, the private schools also have better classrooms and toilets and are better furnished than the public schools. The researchers estimated that at least half of the pupils in the public schools sat on the floor and most of the buildings were dilapidated. The classrooms in four out of the six public schools were in a very bad shape and could be dangerous to pupils' health and safety. However, the public schools were better off than the private schools in terms of availability of a playground: three of the six private schools had no playground at all.

Across the three states and in both public and private schools, parents provide school uniforms and learning materials such as textbooks, exercise books, pens and pencils.

Table 5.8 Pupil enrolment in selected schools

State	Type	School	LGA	P1			P2			P3			P4			P5			P6			TOTAL		
IMO STATE	Public	Dev P, Owerri	Owerri Mun.	71	50	121	28	22	50	19	24	43	22	29	51	24	26	50	25	17	42	168	189	357
		Ikenegbu Lay P	Owerri Mun.	95	110	205	90	140	230	85	150	235	90	150	240	80	155	235	98	105	203	810	538	1,348
		Town, Enyiogugu	Aboh Mbaise	11	4	15	6	5	11	5	8	13	8	4	12	6	6	12	9	7	16	34	45	79
		Eziala Enyiogugu	Aboh Mbaise	10	12	22	15	13	28	9	18	27	20	15	35	25	15	40	28	25	53	98	107	205
		Urban P. Okigwe	Okigwe	11	12	23	11	12	23	14	14	28	15	14	29	12	17	29	14	14	28	83	77	160
		Ilube P	Okigwe	18	14	32	15	24	39	16	19	35	20	24	44	17	20	37	20	28	48	129	106	235
		Total		216	202	418	165	216	381	148	233	381	175	236	411	164	239	403	194	196	390	1,322	1,062	2,384
	Private	St. Juliana NPS	Owerri Mun.	26	38	64	12	36	48	15	42	57	20	37	57	10	39	49	13	35	48	227	96	323
		Christ Church P	Owerri Mun.	24	18	42	26	26	52	25	20	45	17	22	39	16	14	30	13	9	22	109	121	230
		Divine Message Enyiogugu	Aboh Mbaise	11	10	21	11	14	25	14	10	24	8	18	26	10	9	19	16	16	32	77	70	147
		Holy Child Enyiogugu	Aboh Mbaise	15	15	30	15	15	30	18	14	32	19	17	36	19	14	33	-		0	75	86	161
		Excellent Foundation P	Okigwe	30	33	63	21	28	49	20	24	44	16	20	36	10	18	28	12	19	31	142	109	251
		Christ the King P	Okigwe	20	50	70	20	40	60	12	15	27	34	32	66	12	30	42	12	33	45	200	110	310
		Total		126	164	290	105	159	264	104	125	229	114	146	260	77	124	201	66	112	178	830	592	1,422
KADUNA STATE	Public	Mallam Jallo P. Rigachikun	Igabi	184	138	322	162	153	315	159	147	306	119	99	218	103	106	209	83	99	182	742	810	1,552
		LEA Unguwar Tsalha, Rigachikun	Igabi	25	26	51	23	18	41	20	18	38	21	16	37	20	20	40	18	14	32	112	127	239
		LEA P. DarnishiS	Chikun	28	20	48	18	14	32	22	19	41	17	15	32	14	12	26	18	16	34	96	117	213
		LEA P. Bakin Kasuwa	Chikun	22	20	42	25	20	45	25	22	47	19	18	37	20	22	42	21	19	40	121	132	253
		LEA P. Unguwar Rimi	Kaduna N	191	173	364	167	163	330	153	143	296	157	132	289	175	188	363	102	120	222	919	945	1,864
		LEA P. Hayin Banki	Kaduna N	86	85	171	72	68	140	73	65	138	60	55	115	53	50	103	56	54	110	377	400	777
		Total		536	462	998	467	436	903	452	414	866	393	335	728	385	398	783	298	322	620	2,367	2,531	4,898
	Private	Hajiya Ramatu NP, Rigachikun	Igabi	18	15	33	27	23	50	17	19	36	15	10	25	11	22	33	10	11	21	100	98	198
		Hikima NP, Rigachikun	Igabi	14	13	27	20	18	38	17	15	32	14	13	27	14	16	30	13	9	22	84	92	176
		Better Future NP	Chikun	19	15	34	18	15	33	20	18	38	18	13	31	14	12	26	12	11	23	84	101	185
		Jackjum NP	Chikun	15	13	28	21	14	35	14	12	26	15	13	28	17	17	32	17	13	30	82	97	179
		Winners Comprehensive College	Kaduna N	18	21	39	21	19	40	16	22	38	12	15	27	18	16	29	18	12	30	105	98	203
		Grace NP	Kaduna N	19	18	37	15	14	29	22	19	41	17	19	36	12	12	30	17	13	30	95	108	203
		Total		103	95	198	122	103	225	106	105	211	91	83	174	85	95	180	87	69	156	550	594	1,144

OGUN STATE

Category	School	Area	P1			P2			P3			P4			P5			P6			TOTAL		
Public	Baptist NP, Idi aba	Abk Sth	43	57	100	70	58	128	78	81	159	90	103	193	84	64	148	75	75	150	438	440	878
Public	C.A.C. NP, Lantoro	Abk Sth	47	57	104	44	49	93	45	47	92	53	62	115	57	45	102	33	38	71	279	298	577
Public	L.G. P, Arafen	W/side	34	45	79	47	38	85	46	42	88	41	41	82	40	48	88	50	38	88	246	264	510
Public	L.G. P, Ibiade	W/side	69	65	134	66	52	118	60	62	122	50	56	106	48	50	98	49	56	105	349	334	683
Public	Parako United, Igbile	Odogbolu	16	19	35	11	19	30	18	12	30	13	22	35	15	12	27	16	15	31	88	100	188
Public	St. Pauls, Eyin	Odogbolu	5	7	12	4	5	9	7	9	16	6	8	14	4	6	10	6	5	11	32	40	72
Public	Total		214	250	464	242	221	463	254	253	507	253	292	545	248	225	473	233	223	456	1,474	1,434	2,908
Private	Adonia NP, Abeokuta	Abk Sth	13	4	17	10	12	22	8	7	15	13	14	27	3	6	9	13	10	23	57	56	113
Private	Shorem NP, Abeokuta	Abk Sth	15	12	27	11	12	23	10	9	19	11	11	22	11	7	18	8	6	14	66	57	123
Private	Pathfinder NP	W/side	22	18	40	24	19	43	18	13	31	15	13	28	17	16	33	26	21	47	112	110	222
Private	Ansar Sunnah NP	W/side	22	18	40			47			45			40			30			0	87	115	202
Private	Victorious Children	Odogbolu	66	34	100	45	40	85	28	35	63	24	37	61	25	35	60	27	31	58	204	223	427
Private	El-Bethel City NP, Latogun	Kaduna N	9	6	15	8	6	14	8	7	15	6	7	13	12	14	26	4	6	10	41	52	93
Private	Total		92	147	239	114	120	234	86	102	188	101	90	191	88	88	176	77	75	152	567	613	1,180
	Total public		966	914	1,880	874	873	1,747	854	900	1,754	821	863	1,684	797	862	1,659	751	715	1,466	5,163	5,027	10,190
	Total private		376	351	727	382	341	723	332	296	628	319	306	625	307	250	557	256	230	486	1,947	1,799	3,746
	Total public & private		1,342	1,265	2,607	1,255	1,215	2,470	1,232	1,150	2,382	1,182	1,127	2,309	1,169	1,047	2,216	1,007	945	1,952	7,110	6,826	13,936

P = Primary school NP = Nursery & primary school LEA = Local Education Authority

Table 5.9 Number and qualifications of teachers in selected schools

State	Sector	School	Location	Total	PhD	M.Ed	B.Ed	NCE	TC II	OND	School Cert	Others	Pupils	Pupils per teacher (PTR)	Pupils per qualified teacher (PQTR)
IMO STATE	Public	Dev P, Owerri	Owerri Mun.	27			7	20					357	13.2	13.2
		Ikenegbu Lay P	Owerri Mun.	68			51	17					1,348	19.8	19.8
		Town, Enyiogugu	Aboh Mbaise	11			5	6					79	7.2	7.2
		Eziala Enyiogugu	Aboh Mbaise	19			1	18					205	10.8	10.8
		Urban P, Okigwe	Okigwe	9			1	8					160	17.8	17.8
		Ilube P	Okigwe	17			9	1	7				235	13.8	23.5
	Private	St. Juliana NPS	Owerri Mun.	15			3	7	2			3	323	21.5	32.3
		Christ Church P	Owerri Mun.	10			1	6	3				230	23.0	32.9
		Divine Message Enyiogugu	Aboh Mbaise	10				10					147	14.7	14.7
		Holy Child Enyiogugu	Aboh Mbaise	8				5	2			1	161	20.1	32.2
		Excellent Foundation P	Okigwe	14			3	2	8			1	251	17.9	50.2
		Christ the King P	Okigwe	8			3	3	2				310	38.8	51.7
KADUNA STATE	Public	Mallam Jallo P, Rigachikun	Igabi	51			6	32	1			12	1,552	30.4	40.8
		LEA Unguwar Tsalha, Rigachikun	Igabi	17			2	10	2			3	239	14.1	19.9
		LEA P, DamishiS	Chikun	16				5	8			3	213	13.3	42.6
		LEA P, Bakin Kasuwa	Chikun	18				8	7			3	253	14.1	31.6
		LEA P, Unguwar Rimi	Kaduna N	90			4	35	37			14	1,864	20.7	47.8
		LEA P, Hayin Banki	Kaduna N	43			5	22	10			6	777	18.1	28.8
		Total		235	0	0	17	112	65	0	0	41	4,898	20.8	38.0
	Private	Hajiya Ramatu NP, Rigachikun	Igabi	15			8	7					198	13.2	13.2
		Hikima NP, Rigachikun	Igabi	11				8	3				176	16.0	22.0
		Better Future NP	Chikun	10			1	6	3				185	18.5	26.4
		Jackjum NP	Chikun	13				6	4		3		179	13.8	29.8
		Winners Comprehensive College	Kaduna N	8				5	1		2		203	25.4	40.6
		Grace NP	Kaduna N	14			2	8	3	1			203	14.5	20.3
		Total		71	0	0	11	40	14	1	5	0	1,144	16.1	22.4

	School	Location		PhD	M.Ed	B.Ed	NCE	TC II	OND	School Cert	Others		Pupils per teacher (PTR)	Pupils per qualified teacher (PQTR)
Public	Baptist NP, Idi aba	Abk Sth	33			2	31					878	26.6	26.6
	C.A.C. NP, Lantoro	Abk Sth	24		1	4	18	1				577	24.0	25.1
	L.G. P. Arafen	W/side	12			1	8	3				510	42.5	56.7
	L.G. P. Ibiade	W/side	29			10	16	3				683	23.6	26.3
	Parako United, Igbile	Odogbolu	11			3	5	3				188	17.1	23.5
	St. Pauls, Eyin	Odogbolu	7			1	3	3				72	10.3	18.0
Private	Adonia NP, Abeokuta	Abk Sth	12				6	4	1	1		113	9.4	18.8
	Shorem NP, Abeokuta	Abk Sth	9				3	1		5		123	13.7	41.0
	Pathfinder NP	W/side	16			5	9	2				222	13.9	15.9
	Ansar Sunnah NP	W/side	8			1	6	1				202	25.3	28.9
	Victorious Children	Odogbolu	30			2	23	5				427	14.2	17.1
	El Bethel City NP, Latogun	Kaduna N	23		1	7	8	4		3		93	4.0	5.8
Total Public			502	0	1	112	263	85	0	0	41	10,190	20.3	27.1
Total Private			234	0	1	36	128	48	2	14	5	3,746	16.0	22.7

P = Primary school NP = Nursery & primary school LEA = Local Education Authority

This is an anomaly in the case of public schools, because the policy for states is that the government should provide textbooks. These costs are an additional 'hidden' cost of education for parents in both types of schools, not to mention the opportunity cost of sending children to school. The estimated cost of school uniform (for one child), textbooks, exercise books and writing materials is about 4,500 naira (N) per annum[22].

Although the official national policy is that no fees should be charged in any public primary school, the reality is quite different and parents do shoulder a significant proportion of the cost of public schooling.

To get a good picture of the cost structure for private schools, the cost of uniforms, books and writing materials needs to be added to those of school fees and levies.

Table 5.10 Fees charged by selected private schools

				Fee charged (naira)	Levy charged (naira)
IMO STATE	**Private**	St. Juliana NPS		6,600	400
		Christ Church P		3,100	0
		Divine Mercy Enyiogugu		1,800	200
		Holy Child Enyiogugu		2,000	300
		Excellent Foundation P		2,700	0
		Christ the King P		4,500	0
		Average		**3,450**	**150**
KADUNA STATE	**Private**	Hajiya Ramatu NP, Rigachikun	class 1-3:	4,050	700
			class 4-6:	4,800	700
		Hikima NP, Rigachikun		4,000	350
		Better Future NP		3,500	300
		Jackjum NP		2,500	350
		Winners Comprehensive College	class 1-3:	4,050	600
			class 4-6:	4,800	600
		Grace NP		5,000	1,000
		Average		**4,088**	**575**
OGUN STATE	**Private**	Adonia NP, Abeokuta		3,000	0
		Shokem NP, Abeokuta		2,500	1000
		Pathfinder NP		3,000	500
		Ansar Sunnah NP		3,000	0
		Victorious Children		2,000	1000
		El Bethel City NP, Latogun		2,500	500
P = Primary school NP = Nursery & primary school LEA = Local Education Authority					

Table 5.10 shows that only five of the 18 private schools surveyed do not charge a levy. Levies are usually tied to a specific activity or a project: for example, Devine Mercy and Holy Child schools in Imo state stated that their levies were for extra classes and to fund the PTA respectively. Should a school wish to undertake a project or activity that cannot be funded from the fees, a special levy could be imposed to enable the school to carry out the project.

Levies are usually determined jointly by the PTA and the school management. In all the public and private schools sampled for this study, there exists a fairly strong and cordial relationship between the PTA and the school management.

In Kaduna state, four out of five public school PTAs are dormant. The PTAs in the private schools, on the other hand, meet at least once a term and take far-reaching decisions on matters affecting the school and contribute materially and morally to the development of the school.

In Ogun state, the levies contain a N200–300 charge that goes toward funding the PTA. The PTAs are members of the School Advisory Committee in all the selected private schools, thus making them part of the decision-making process. Discussions with the head teachers, teachers and the PTA indicated that the Advisory Committee's advice and decisions are generally taken seriously and fully implemented. However, in the public schools, the PTA's support to the schools is generally restricted to provision of furniture, repair of damaged buildings, fencing and the provision of computers and does not extend to decision-making and planning. In public schools, decisions are taken centrally by the LGA and the state government.

Focus group discussions with teachers

Focus group discussions were held with the teachers in both the public and private schools on a wide range of issues. Table 5.11, below, summarises their responses and the case study findings.

Table 5.11 Teachers' responses to focus groups questions

Questions for teachers	Private			Public		
	Yes	No	Total	Yes	No	Total
Do Teachers receive an annual leave grant or bonus?	0	72	72	72	0	72
Are there well-defined criteria for staff promotion?	0	72	72	72	0	72
Do teachers have opportunities to attend seminars, workshop etc?	24	48	72	61	11	72
Are there clearly-defined staff development policies?	0	72	72	42	30	72
Does the school have a PTA?	72	0	72	56	16	72
Do parents visit the school?	60	12	72	22	50	72
Are Parents involved in the affairs of school?	64	8	72	51	21	72

Private schools tend to be worse off than public schools in terms of payment of an annual leave grants to teachers, staff promotion and opportunities for continuing professional development.[23] Public schools, unlike private schools, do have well-defined staff development policies that are centrally determined by the state. However, although these policies exist, their implementation is patchy. There is greater accountability in private schools, because parents take an interest and get involved in the school's day-to-day affairs. Parents who have children in private schools do in fact hold the school and teachers accountable for their children's academic performance in general and their performance in high-stake public examinations in particular. This contrasts, in particular, with the large number of public schools whose PTAs are largely inactive.

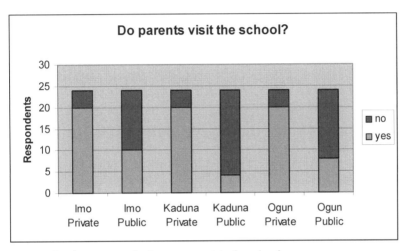

Figure 5.1 Teachers' views on whether parents visit the school

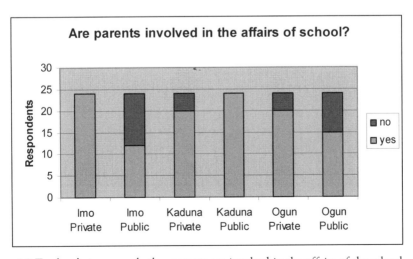

Figure 5.2 Teachers' views on whether parents are involved in the affairs of the school

Figures 5.1 and 5.2, above, demonstrate teachers' responses to two questions in the three states. From these responses, it appears that fewer parents visit public schools than private ones, but teachers still claim that parents are involved in the running of public schools nonetheless.

Teachers' pay

Table 5.12, below, displays details of teachers' pay in those schools where this information was available. Where average teachers' pay was given as a range of values, these are displayed in the right-hand column. These figures do not include an estimation of the number of teachers on each salary. The data is therefore included only for illustrative purposes to demonstrate that the rough average monthly salary for a teacher in a private school is markedly lower than in a public school. Furthermore, public schoolteachers in Kaduna state are paid far less than their counterparts in other states. In fact, Kaduna state government pays the lowest salary in the whole of Nigeria.

Teaching and learning aids

In all three states, private schools have better teaching and learning aids than public schools. This includes widespread use of wall charts, maps, diagrams, pictures, counters and audio-cassettes that are directly relevant to the school curriculum. This compares markedly with the bare walls of classrooms in public schools.

Teacher attendance

Teacher attendance was comparatively higher in private than in public schools in all three states. The recorded level of teacher absenteeism (for whatever reason) in Imo state was about 7 per cent in private schools as compared with 10–20 per cent in the public schools. In Kaduna and Ogun, this figure was less than 5 per cent as compared with 15–20 per cent in the public schools.

Performance in public examinations

Comparative data on the relative performance of public and private schools in examinations in the three states could not be obtained from the authorities. Based on the information provided by teachers, head teachers and parents, pupils from both private and public schools do well in the common entrance examination into JSS. However, this is not a good measure of quality or performance, because marks are often inflated and the selection process into the best JSS is beset with corruption. All the private schools in Ogun organise special classes to prepare pupils for the common entrance examination.

Table 5.12 Teachers' salaries in selected schools

IMO STATE	Public	Dev P, Owerri		
		Ikenegbu Lay P		
		Town, Enyiogugu		
		Eziala Enyiogugu		
		Urban P, Okigwe		
		Ilube P		
		Average	**20,000**	**8,000-32,000**
	Private	St. Juliana NPS	11,250	7,500-15,000
		Christ Church P	6,500	
		Divine Mercy Enyiogugu	5,000	
		Holy Child Enyiogugu	4,500	3,000-6,000
		Excellent Foundation P	5,000	
		Christ the King P	7,800	
KADUNA STATE	Public	Mallam Jallo P, Rigachikun		
		LEA Unguwar Tsalha, Rigachikun		
		LEA P, DamishiS		
		LEA P, Bakin Kasuwa		
		LEA P, Unguwar Rimi		
		LEA P, Hayin Banki		
		Average	**15,750**	**6,500-25,000**
	Private	Hajiya Ramatu NP, Rigachikun	4,500	
		Hikima NP, Rigachikun	4,000	
		Better Future NP	3,500	
		Jackjum NP	3,000	
		Winners Comprehensive College	5,000	
		Grace NP	5,000	
		Average	**4,167**	
OGUN STATE	Public	Baptist NP, Idi aba		
		C.A.C. NP, Lantoro		
		L.G. P, Arafen		
		L.G. P, Ibiade		
		Parako United, Igbile		
		St. Pauls, Eyin		
		Average	**20,250**	**8,500-32,000**
	Private	Adonia NP, Abeokuta	3,000	
		Shokem NP, Abeokuta	5,000	
		Pathfinder NP	10,000	
		Ansar Sunnah NP	8,000	
		Victorious Children	7,000	
		El Bethel City NP, Latogun	6,500	
		Average	**6,583**	
			18,667	
			5,808	

P = Primary school NP = Nursery & primary school LEA = Local Education Authority

Focus group discussions with parents

In each school, focus group discussions with parents were held. These discussions focused on the following:

- Why they chose to send their children to this particular school;
- The fees and levies they pay and whether they get 'value for money';
- The support they provide to the schools;
- The school's academic performance as compared with other schools in the locality; and
- Teacher attendance and performance.

The most often cited reasons for choice of school by parents who have children in private schools are:

- Proximity to the home;
- Greater teacher commitment and dedication, as indicated by comparatively lower levels of teacher absenteeism;
- That the fees charged are reasonable and affordable;
- The quality of the school is better than that of other schools in the locality;
- There is a high level of discipline and pupils in the school are 'morally upright'; and
- The head teacher is good and manages the school very well.

According to all the parents of the selected private schools, the fees charged by the schools are reasonable and affordable and they do not feel they are being exploited by the owner/proprietor. On the contrary, the proprietors are very flexible in terms of giving parents sufficient time to pay. They all felt that they were 'getting value for money'. In Imo, parents also support the schools by contributing funds for the repair or construction of classrooms or offices, and for the provision or repair of furniture. In Ogun, parents support the school in the form of payment of levies for specific projects and advising the school on specific issues relating to the administration of the school and pupils' discipline. They reported being satisfied with the teachers' level of dedication and commitment and the teaching and learning that takes place in the schools as compared with public schools.

A comment from a peasant farmer sending his children to private school in Kaduna:

'The fees are not too high and are comparable to what similar schools charge as fees. If you say the fees are too high and we are being exploited, then I will want you to answer this question: is it not better to pay the fees even if they are exorbitant (which in our case is not true) than to take my child to the so-called free, non-fee paying schools where the children are not taught anything? I have two children in this school and before I transferred them from the LEA school to this school they could not write even their names correctly... Now they can read and write. So which is better for me?'

Parents were also asked to express their satisfaction or dissatisfaction on a number of issues. The table below summarises their responses.

Overall, parents with children attending private schools are more satisfied than those with children attending public schools. Indeed, private schools scored better than public in all categories. The teaching and learning facilities and parents having to contribute to the repair of damaged or old buildings was the greatest source of dissatisfaction for parents in private schools. These were also the greatest sources of dissatisfaction in the public schools, along with the financial contribution that parents have to make to the school. Figures 5.3 and 5.4 below demonstrate that proportionately fewer parents of children in public schools in Imo and Kaduna were satisfied with the level of financial support they provide to the school and with the teaching and learning facilities.

Parents of children in public schools generally expressed satisfaction with teacher performance. This is in spite of teacher absenteeism running as high as 20 per cent in Imo and 25 per cent in Ogun in some of the sampled schools.

Parents were also asked to say what were the strengths and weaknesses of their schools. The most often cited strengths of private schools were the high pupil-teacher ratio (PTR) and highly-committed and dedicated teachers who, unlike their public school counterparts, do not go on strike because they are not unionised. The most

Table 5.13 Parents' responses to focus group questions

Questions for teachers Are you satisfied with the following:	Private			Public		
	Yes	No	Total	Yes	No	Total
Teachers' attendance?	90	0	90	80	10	90
Teachers' performance?	87	3	90	75	15	90
Pupil performance?	88	2	90	67	23	90
Teaching and learning facilities?	74	16	90	41	49	90
Level of discipline among pupils?	83	7	90	69	21	90
Teachers' attitudes towards parents?	86	4	90	74	16	90
Financial support by parents to the school?	85	5	90	34	56	90
Repair of damaged or old buildings by parents?	73	16	90	39	51	90
Getting value for money, i.e. is the expenditure on fees, levies and other costs incurred worth it?	87	3	90	66	24	90
Relationship between school and PTA?	90	0	90	77	13	90
Total	843	56	900	622	278	900

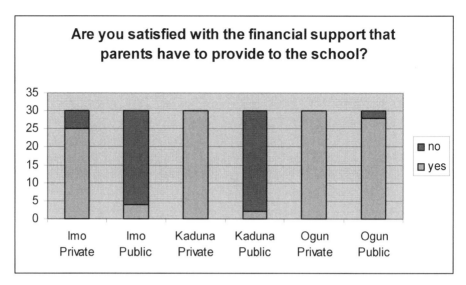

Figure 5.3 Parent satisfaction with the financial support they have to provide

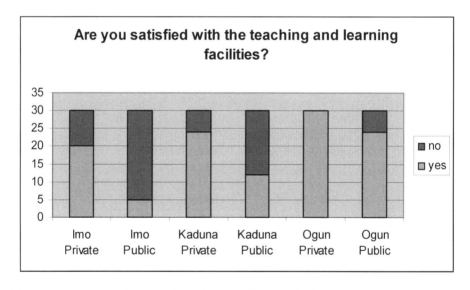

Figure 5.4 Parent satisfaction with teaching and learning facilities

commonly-cited strengths of the public schools, on the other hand, were availability and adequacy of qualified teachers, availability of space for sports, greater emphasis on religious and moral education and regular inspection by government education inspectors.

The weaknesses of private schools were reported to be a shortage of sufficient facilities for sports and a lack of adequate space for expanding the school facilities. The public school weaknesses, meanwhile, were their inadequate classrooms and furniture and poor maintenance.

Parents were also asked to say whether the schools attended by their children are getting better or worse in terms of teachers' performance, academic performance of pupils, school discipline and teaching-learning facilities. Figures 5.5 to 5.9, below, display the results broken down across the three states.

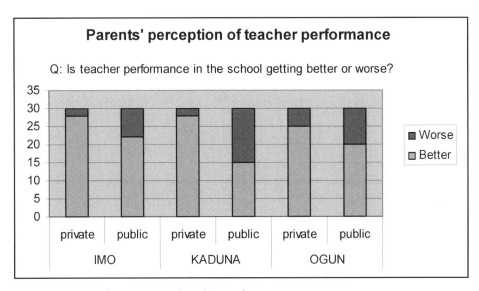

Figure 5.5 Parents' perception of teacher performance

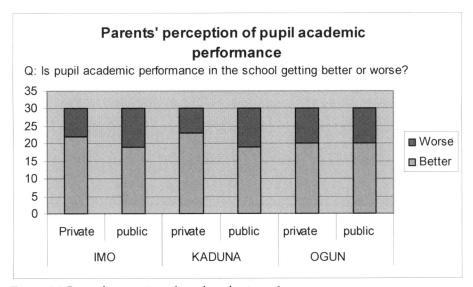

Figure 5.6 Parents' perception of pupil academic performance

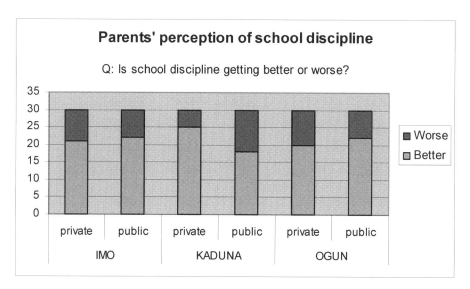

Figure 5.7 Parents' perception of school discipline

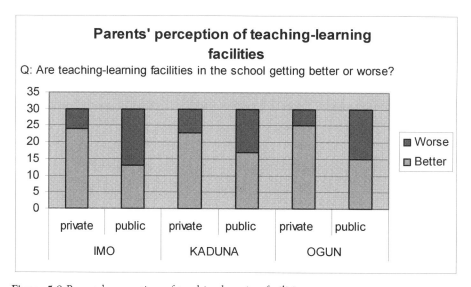

Figure 5.8 Parents' perception of teaching-learning facilities

The figures above show that there are significant differences in the responses of parents across the three states. On grounds of teacher performance and teaching-learning facilities, it is clear that parents judge private schools to be doing better than public schools. Public schools across all three states fair particularly poorly on teaching-learning facilities. The other two grounds for assessment, pupil academic performance and school discipline, are less conclusive.

Low-cost Private Education

Owners of private schools

Discussions with owners of private schools focused on the problems they faced, their plans for the future and how government can support them to contribute more effectively to the attainment of the Education for All (EFA) goal. The major problems owners identified were: difficulties in trying to acquire land for school expansion; late payment of fees by parents; undue harassment by government officials with regards to the implementation of the new minimum standards for basic education; lack of sufficient classrooms; the high level of teacher attrition; and multiple taxation by both the state and local government.

Each proprietor was also asked to say what his/her future plans were. The most common aspirations were:

- to acquire land and build a permanent site; and

- to build more classrooms and thereby significantly raise enrolments.

Other common aspirations included procuring computers, setting up a secondary school section so that all graduates of primary could transit into secondary, organising in-house seminars and workshops for staff and purchasing a school van.

All the proprietors expressed the opinion that demand for private education will continue to grow, because of increasing dissatisfaction with the quality of public school tuition and industrial action in public primary schools, which lead to frequent and lengthy closures of schools. They also expressed the view that government should not ignore the contributions of private schools to the attainment of the goal of Universal Primary Education (UPE). Indeed, the proprietors felt that the government should support them with grants and help them to acquire land onto which they could expand their facilities and thereby increase their enrolment. Another form of assistance they said private schoolteachers are currently excluded from is the ongoing teacher re-training programme under the MDG project.

Focus group discussion with local government authority secretaries and Nigeria Union of Teachers (NUT)

Discussions with local government authority (LGA) secretaries and NUT chairs focused on the following issues:

- Number of private schools in their LGA;

- Whether there was any state or LGA law on private schools which guides their relationship with such schools;

- The activities of the Association of Private School Proprietors in the LGA;

- The role of private schools in providing access to primary education; and

- The quality of tuition provided by private schools as compared with public schools.

In Imo state, the education secretaries said that there were 19 registered/government-recognised private schools in Owerri Municipal LGA and nine in both Aboh Mbaise LGA and Okigwe LGA. However, they believed that the number of unregistered and unrecognised primary schools is higher than that of registered/recognised schools. The estimated number of unregistered/ unrecognised schools in Owerri Municipal LGA is at least 25, while in Mbaise LGA and Okigwe LGA the estimated figures were 10 and 15 respectively. However, more accurate figures will be obtained in due course when the ongoing attempt to register or close down all unregistered schools in the state is completed. Attempts were being made by the Ministry of Education, the State Universal Basic Education Board and the LGAs to register all schools in the state and ensure that only schools that meet the prescribed minimum standards are allowed to operate. Eleven of 19 private schools in Owerri Municipal are owned by individuals, compared to three out of six in Mbaise LGA and four out of nine in Okigwe LGA. The remainder are owned by the church, NGOs or local communities. However, all the private schools depend on fees and levies for their operations, irrespective of their mode of ownership and management.

According to the education secretaries, there were 62 private schools in Kaduna North LGA, 17 in Igabi LGA and 12 in Chikun LGA. However, they pointed out that the census of both registered and unregistered schools was still going on and these figures will change when it is completed. When asked to estimate the total number of unregistered schools, they informed the researchers that they believed that there were more unregistered/unrecognised schools than registered/recognised schools. The unregistered schools are not included in official statistics.

In Ogun state, the education secretaries said that there were 102 private schools in Abeokuta South and North LGAs, seven in Ogun waterside and 30 in Odogbolu. Further questions revealed that these figures include both registered/recognised schools and unregistered/unrecognised schools. More than 50 per cent of the schools in Abeokuta North and South and Odogbolu LGAs are unregistered/unrecognised and therefore not included in the official statistics. More than two-thirds of the schools are owned by private individuals, with the rest owned by religious organisations and communities.

A directorate of private schools was established in Nigeria's Ministry of Education in May 2007. Its main objective is to generate reliable data on all aspects of private schooling and also to develop guidelines for the assessment of the quality of private schools and regulate and control their activities. The directorate should also collaborate with the Association of Private School Proprietors in order to promote the enhancement of quality and standards in private schools.

The legal framework for the assessment and regulation of private schools in all three states is the Private Education (Miscellaneous Provisions) Edict No. 10 of 1989, particularly Appendix D part 3 entitled 'Opening and Closing of Schools and Institutions', and also circulars and guidelines on the establishment of schools issued by the Ministry of Education and the State Universal Basic Education Board. The

Association of Proprietors of Private Schools ensures that its members are aware of and understand the edict and the circulars and guidelines issued by the authorities.

The Local Government Education Authority (LGEA) secretaries and the NUT Chairs in the selected LGAs have a very positive attitude towards private education and the potentials of private schools in facilitating Nigeria's attainment of the EFA and MDG targets. A good summary of their views would be something like this: 'Government cannot do it alone. We must all join hands to ensure that all our children have access to education. Government, the private sector, philanthropists, religious organisations, communities etc. must work together to provide education to all our citizens. Government does not have the money to do it alone.' What worries them is the quality of private schools. They are of the view that the quality of tuition provided in private primary schools is generally inferior to the quality of tuition in public schools. According to them, most if not all private schools employ teachers who do not possess the minimum teaching qualification (i.e. NCE), so as to reduce costs and increase their profit margins. The salary they pay is below the level prescribed for teachers and in most cases just about one-third of what teachers in public schools are paid. The NUT is currently compiling data on this and will make a formal submission to the National Council on Education and urge it to take action against schools that underpay teachers.[24] Unless these schools are properly controlled and regulated, the secretaries and NUT Chairs believe they will continue to employ unqualified teachers and provide substandard/low-quality education.

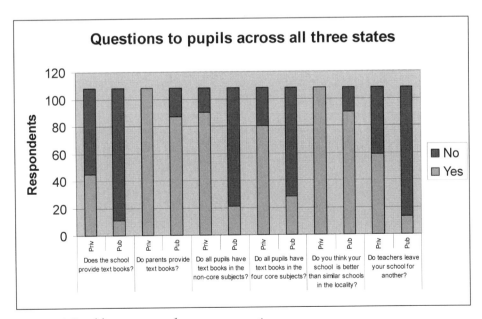

Figure 5.9 Pupils' responses to focus group questions

Table 5.14 Pupils' responses to focus group questions

Questions for pupils	IMO STATE						KADUNA STATE						OGUN STATE					
	Private			Public			Private			Public			Private			Public		
	Yes	No	Total	Yes	No	Total	Yes	No	Total	Yes	No	Total	Yes	No	Total	Yes	No	Total
Do you like your school?	36	0	36	36	0	36	36	0	36	36	0	36	36	0	36	36	0	36
Are the teachers punctual?	36	0	36	36	0	36	36	0	36	36	0	36	36	0	36	36	0	36
Are the teachers willing to teach and committed?	36	0	36	36	0	36	36	0	36	36	0	36	36	0	36	36	0	36
Has there been any physical assault on pupils by teachers?	0	36	36	0	36	36	0	36	36	0	36	36	0	36	36	0	36	36
Has there been sexual abuse by teachers?	0	36	36	0	36	36	0	36	36	0	36	36	0	36	36	0	36	36
Does the school provide textbooks?*	10	26	36	6	30	36	15	21	36	4	32	36	20	16	36	1	35	36
Do parents provide textbooks?	36	0	36	29	7**	36	36	0	36	30	6	36	36	0	36	28	8**	36
Are teachers regularly in school?	36	0	36	36	0	36	36	0	36	26	10	36	36	0	36	36	0	36
Do all pupils have textbooks in non-core subjects?	30	6	36	7	29	36	28	8	36	6	30	36	32	4	36	8	28	36
Do all pupils have textbooks in the four core subjects?***	26	10	36	9	27	36	27	9	36	9	27	36	27	9	36	10	26	36
Do you think your school is better than similar schools in the locality?	36	0	36	28	8	36	36	0	36	32	4	36	36	0	36	30	6	36
Do teachers leave your school for another?	24	12	36	4	32	36	9	27	36	3	33	36	26	10	36	6	30	36
Do pupils transfer from your school to another?	2	34	36	5	31	30	4	32	36	9	27	36	0	36	36	3	33	36

*Although parents are required to buy textbooks for their children/wards, the school has a limited number of the textbooks that children whose parents have not yet bought the books can share in class.

**This is simply an inaccurate perception. Parents are responsible for buying textbooks for their children, even in public schools.

***English, maths, science and social studies.

From the table above, it can be seen that pupils unanimously say that they like their schools, their teachers are punctual and they believe them to be willing to teach and committed. Furthermore, none of these pupils reported physical assault or sexual abuse by teachers.

Focus group discussion with pupils

Focus group discussions were held with the pupils in both the public and private schools on a wide range of issues. Table 5.14 summarises their responses and the case study findings.

Figure 5.9 on p. 123 demonstrates some of the pupils' responses to questions in graphic form across the three states. From this it seems that fewer public schools provide textbooks. Marginally more parents of children in private schools provide textbooks than in public schools. The combination of these two factors may in part lead to the large proportions of pupils who said that they do not have textbooks in either the core or non-core subjects. It is also interesting that significantly more pupils from private schools said that teachers leave their school to transfer to another.

Pupils were also asked to specify what they liked about their respective schools. Their responses are summarised in Table 5.15.

The dominant forms of punishment in both public and private schools are caning, 'being made to kneel down for long periods' and 'hard labour' such as field clearing, sweeping and cutting grass.

Summary of findings on the case studies

- Data from the three case studies indicated that the total enrolment in the selected public and private schools was 13,936, of which 3,746 pupils (26.9 per cent) were enrolled in private schools. Thus the private schools' share of enrolment is relatively high at nearly one third of total enrolment. This figure is quite impressive and underlines the contribution of private schools to EFA.

Table 5.15 What pupils like about their school

Private	Public
The teachers teach well	The teachers teach well
There are not too many pupils	The school has many qualified teachers
The school is clean	There is a playground to play football
The headmaster is very friendly	The pupils are well-behaved
Pupils do very well in the state's common entrance exam	The school is not far from home
The school teaches computer skills	
The school is not far from home	
Pupils like their uniform	
The school environment is beautiful	

- In Kaduna and Ogun states there were no significant gender differences in enrolment between public and private schools. However, this was not the case in Imo state where more girls than boys were enrolled in both public and private schools.

- The selected private schools had better PTRs and PQTRs than their public-school counterparts. They also had relatively better classroom facilities and make greater use of improvised audio-visual materials than the public schools.

- In all the states and LGAs covered in this study, government officials, the NUT and other stakeholders had a positive attitude towards private schools as contributors to the attainment of EFA targets, even though there was also some concern about the quality of tuition provided in some of the private schools.

- There was a consensus among the officials of the ministries of education, the State Universal Basic Education Boards, the NUT and proprietors of private schools that there were more unregistered and unrecognised schools than government-recognised, registered schools. Estimates ranged from 30 to 50 per cent more unregistered/unrecognised schools than registered, recognised schools.

- Teachers in private schools are more dedicated, committed and are held more accountable for pupils' performance by parents and the schools' management than their counterparts in public schools.

- Teachers in public schools are paid better salaries than teachers in private schools. The salary paid by private schools was extremely low vis-à-vis the approved government rates in the three sampled states. Teachers' conditions of service in private schools are poorer than those of teachers in public schools.

- The fees charged by private schools in the three sampled states varied, but did not exceed N6,600 per term. (Imo: N1,800–N6,600; Kaduna: N2,500–5,000; and Ogun N2,000–N3,000).[25] In addition to fees, parents also pay levies and buy uniforms, textbooks, exercise books and writing materials for their children. This constitutes an additional cost for private schooling, which costs parents an estimated N4,500 per annum.

- Despite the rhetoric of intent of all three tiers of government in the three sampled states, primary education is not free in public schools. In all the three states, parents buy uniforms, textbooks, exercise books and writing materials for their children. These cost an estimated N4,500 per annum and constitute one of the hidden costs of public primary schooling.

- The main reasons parents of children in private schools gave for their choice of school included:

  - Proximity to the home;

  - Greater teacher commitment and dedication, as indicated by comparatively lower levels of teacher absenteeism;

- That the head teacher manages the school well;
- The fees charged are reasonable and affordable;
- The quality of the school is better than that of other schools in the locality; and
- There is a high level of discipline and pupils in the school are 'morally upright.'

All the proprietors of private schools were optimistic that the private education sector would continue to grow, largely as a result of widespread dissatisfaction with the quality of public schools and the inability of government to build enough schools to sufficiently address the social demand for education among the poor. The major elements of their future plans included: the need to acquire land for the building of more classrooms and raising pupil enrolments; the need to establish a secondary school section so as to facilitate ease of transition to JSS for graduates of the primary school section; and the re-training of teachers so as to enhance their classroom performance.

Conclusions and recommendations

It is quite clear that private schools do provide access to education for children in poor urban districts and rural areas. If their potentials are properly harnessed, such schools can help facilitate the attainment of EFA and MDGs on the provision of universal primary education of good quality. The policy implication of this is that these schools, whether registered or unregistered, cannot be ignored. The current policy of closing down the latter can be counter-productive in so far as the emergence of these schools is the direct consequence of the failure of public schools to provide access to good quality primary education to an increasing number of poor people. The National Policy on Education recognises government's inability to shoulder the burden of providing primary education without support from communities and individuals. It also recognises the important role the private sector can play in the provision of better access to education:

'Government welcomes the contributions of voluntary agencies, communities and private individuals in the establishment and management of primary schools alongside those provided by the state and local governments as long as they meet the minimum standards laid down by the federal government... Government regards private participation in education as a way of providing variety and allowing for healthy competition between private and public sectors education [sic]. Government also believes in cost-sharing for the funding of education with genuine voluntary agencies and individuals who, like government, should not run private schools essentially for monetary gains but purely as a humanitarian/social service. Government therefore welcomes the contributions of all interested organisations and agencies.'[26]

The implementation of this policy has in practice violated its spirit. Government has so far focused not on supporting low-cost private schools (e.g. through matching grants, provision of instructional materials), but on intimidating their owners and threatening them with closure on the pretext that they do not meet the prescribed minimum standards for the establishment of schools and are therefore of poor quality. This approach is unhelpful and even hypocritical, since many government-owned schools are also of very poor quality but are not threatened with closure. If there is to be a sincere implementation of the policy, then the state and local governments should begin to see low-cost private schools as partners in the current national efforts to attain the EFA and MDG targets by 2015.

In order to harness the potentials of low-cost private schools in the context of EFA and MDG targets, the following recommendations should be implemented:

- A nationwide census should be conducted of private schools, not only for the purpose of controlling and regulating them but more importantly so as to determine their number, ownership and location, the number of children enrolled in such schools (by gender), the facilities they have and their problems and needs. The census will provide the requisite data for any planned intervention in and provision of support for low-cost private schools.

- Government should, in consultation with stakeholders in the education sector, develop and implement criteria for supporting low-cost private schools, particularly how such schools can benefit from the federal government's UPE intervention fund. This fund is shared to all the 36 states and the FCT every quarter for the purposes of providing instructional materials, construction of classrooms and teacher development. To date, only public schools benefit from the UPE fund. Given the overwhelming evidence that low-cost private schools do provide access to education for the poor, they should also benefit from the fund.

The inspectorate services should be strengthened (in terms of funding, personnel, training and equipment) so as to enable them to monitor the quality of both public and private schools effectively. There should be a paradigm shift from the prevailing view of inspection as a punitive exercise, to one that is advisory, facilitative and formative, and seeks not merely to enforce standards, but more importantly promotes the improvement of all aspects of a school.

Notes

1. Both *Basic and Senior Secondary Education Statistics in Nigeria: 2004 and 2005* and the EMIS data were based on the nationwide school census conducted in February 2005. Data analysis and entry in respect of the 2006 census was still ongoing at time of writing.
2. Federal Ministry of Education (2006).
3. Tooley (2005a), p. ii.
4. Ibid., p. iii.

5. Tooley, J & Dixon, P (2006).

6. Ibid.

7. Ibid., p. 454.

8. Tooley, J (2006).

9. Adediran (2007).

10. Adelabu, M and Rose, P (2004).

11. Ibid.

12. Ibid., p. 65.

13. This is one of the states sampled for this study. The other sampled states are Imo (233 private schools) and Kaduna (373 private schools).

14. Federal Ministry of Education (2006).

15. Ibid.

16. Federal Ministry of Education (2005).

17. Ibid., p. 45.

18. The national mean score is on p.43, paragraph 1 of the MLA report and is not shown in the table.

19. Ibid., based on the data on pp. 121–200.

20. Ibid.

21. Federal Ministry of Education (2006) and Department of Planning Research & Statistics, Kaduna State Ministry of Education.

22. Taking £1.00 to be N232.40 as at January 2008.

23. This is not based on actual classroom performance. The most important criteria are length of service/waiting period and 'good conduct.'

24. The National Council on Education is the highest policy-making organisation in the country and is chaired by the Minister of Education. Its members include all the state Commissioners of Education. Federal and state Directors of Education, heads of education parastatals and agencies, and NGOs also attend all the Council's meetings.

25. Where £1 was equivalent to N232.40 in January 2008.

26. Federal Ministry of Education (2004).

6

UGANDA

Simon Kisira

Introduction

Government's efforts to increase access

With the introduction of the Universal Primary Education (UPE) programme in 1997, primary school enrolment in Uganda increased from 2.9 million (m) in 1996 to 7.3m in 2003. About 50 per cent of the lowest economic quartile was enrolled in 1992, while by 1999, 83.7 per cent of children of school-going age were enrolled. It is asserted that the majority of the 23 per cent of the Ugandan population benefiting from primary education are from the lowest income quartile. The 2001 Uganda Demographic Household Survey (UDHS) indicated that 24 per cent of children were out of school because of monetary cost. Public intervention was thus said to raise access and equity. In addition, the UPE policy of enrolling all children of school-going age had the effect of increasing girls' enrolment to about 50 per cent of total enrolment, thus significantly reducing the gender-parity gap.[1] However, the contribution of private sector education provisions in increasing access, although acknowledged, is not fully known.

Completion rates in the primary sub-sector are still very low in Uganda – averaging 22 per cent. An enormous amount of public funding is required if the Millennium Development Goal (MDG) of children completing a full course of primary education is to be attained. It is also estimated that government requires building an average of 100,000 classrooms per year in order to attain the desired teacher-classroom ratio of 1:1. Projections show that government is only able to build about 6,000–8,000 classrooms per year over the next two decades.[2]

The above scenario suggests that the current and potential role of private sector in meeting the education-provision gap is obvious. At the advent of UPE, government funded a large number of private schools in peri-urban and rural areas for about four years – providing UPE funds and meeting teachers' remuneration. However, as classroom construction continued in government/government-aided schools using the School Facilities Grants (SFGs), most private schools lost this funding. Consequently, the condition earlier imposed by government of charging not more than 10,000[3] Uganda shillings (USh) per school term was broken with the majority now charging at least USh25,000.[4]

The high dropout rate recorded in primary schools poses a threat to achieving the MDG on education in Uganda. It was observed, for example, that out of the 2.1m pupils enrolled in primary 1 (P1, grade or class 1) in 1997, roughly 33 per cent reached primary 6 by 2002 and 22 per cent reached primary 7 in 2003. The high school dropout rates are attributed to lack of provision of midday meals and parents being poor and unable to afford basic requirements like pens, pencils, books and uniforms.[5] Paradoxically, some of the children who drop out of UPE schools enrol in low-cost private schools and pay tuition fees, albeit in material form sometimes, such as a number of kilos of maize seeds and/or beans.

Uganda's Education Management Information System (EMIS) data for 2006 shows that there are many districts where the net enrolment ratio (NER) is above 100 per cent. There are several suggested reasons for this. One is that the advent of UPE saw many over-age and under-age children enrolled in UPE, who reported their ages to be in the school-going age range of 6–12 years, hence the apparent excessive NER. Another is that the nearly absent provision of Early Childhood Development (ECD) services, especially in rural communities, saw a large cross-section of under-age children enrolled in primary schools.[6] A third possible reason is that on top of the refugee community who send their children to Ugandan schools, there was also an influx of children living in districts bordering Uganda who were attracted across the border by the offer of free education. Other explanations point to cases of deliberate inflation of enrolment figures by head teachers of government schools, so as to attract bigger school capitation grants, given that the allocation of capitation grants is calculated on the basis of school enrolment. Double-counts as a result of transfer-ins and transfer-outs and inter-district movements/displacements – some of them fuelled by insecurity – could also have contributed to this phenomenon. Notwithstanding these different hypotheses, however, the phenomenon of the NER being greater than 100 per cent inevitably casts doubt on the quality and accuracy of EMIS data. The quality, quantity and accuracy of data on private education provisions, for example, may be found wanting.

A policy for disadvantaged children is in place and provides for the provision of basic education for children who are experiencing barriers to education to learning, either outside or within the formal system. The policy is meant to ensure that provisions are in place for multi-grade teaching as a way of reaching isolated communities and providing them with basic education. This includes the provision of incentives for teachers in hard-to-reach areas, the promotion of double-shift teaching as a means to overcoming large teacher-pupil ratios, and measures to enrol orphans and address the learning needs of teachers and children affected by HIV/AIDS. With the exception of the Presidential Initiative on AIDS Strategy for Communication to Youth (PIASCY) – a programme focusing on HIV/AIDS in schools, in which all schools have school assemblies, 'talking compounds' etc. focusing on HIV/AIDS – 'implementation of the policy for disadvantaged children does not seem to have started'. The little known role of private schools in increasing access among disadvantaged children,

Low-cost Private Education

especially in remote, hard-to-reach communities, could provide policy directions. Recognising and supporting these efforts may pay dividends.[7]

While EMIS had shown that over 200,000 children were attending non-formal education in programmes such as Complementary Opportunities for Primary Education (COPE), Alternative Basic Education for Karamoja (ABEK) and Basic Education in Urban Poor Areas (BEUPA), the costed policy framework captured in the Medium-Term Budget Framework (MTBF) of 2003/04 only recognised 67,500 children. There were complications in the manner in which all these children would benefit from UPE capitation grants at district and school levels. Although the MTBF provided for certain aspects of the major non-formal education provisions, the broader costings for disadvantaged children, for example children in hard-to-reach areas, conflict areas of Northern Uganda and internally-displaced people (IDP), as defined in the Strategy for Educationally Disadvantaged Children, were not incorporated into the MTBF.[8]

Furthermore, the education sector review noted that the proposed allocation for School Facilities Grant budget allocation to districts did not cater for internally-displaced pupils, out-of-school children and pupils studying in 'temporary' structures, amongst others. The education planning and review documents, such as the *Ninth Education Review: Aide Memoire* (Ministry of Education and Sports [MoES], 2003) made no mention of private education provisions – suggesting that the review could have entirely focused on public and government-aided education provisions.[9]

In 1999–2002, total government spending on the primary education sub-sector was estimated to be about 68 per cent of overall national expenditure on education.[10] The Indicative Medium-Term Expenditure Framework for the financial years 2003/04–2006/07 placed total expenditure on the education sub-sector (including donor and projects) at USh723.87 billion in financial year 2006/07, with primary education teachers' wages projected at USh258.12 billion (35 per cent of the education total, October 2003) and primary education conditional grants and district development grants estimated at USh47.90 billion and USh65.2 billion respectively.[11] Uganda's Education Bill (2002) outlines the financial responsibility of government in grant-aided education institutions as: ensuring that trained teachers are deployed; paying salaries and allowances to teachers; paying salaries and wages to established non-teaching staff; and paying all statutory grants in the form of aid, including annual recurrent and capitation grants, salaries and wages, capitation and instructional materials. Expenditures by private education providers are not reflected in most government records and yet could be a potentially useful guide in resource allocations and re-prioritisation. Additionally, allocation of public funds to private education providers with regards to their current and potential roles, especially in improving access for disadvantaged children, could be invaluable in the pursuit of the MDG on education.

Education in Uganda at a glance

Education Profile of Uganda
(all figures extrapolated for the year 2007)[12]

- Population of Uganda: 28 million
- School-age population (aged 6–12): 6,384,675
- Gross enrolment rate: 96 per cent
- Total number of primary school pupils: 6,149,067
- Number of primary school pupils in unsubsidised (non-government) schools: 514,454
- Percentage of pupils in unsubsidised schools: 8.4 per cent
- Between 2000 and 2001, government ownership of primary schools increased from 69.7 per cent to 74.8 per cent owing to the initiative to improve equity, whereby government takes over management of community schools
- Over the same period, the private sector nearly doubled its share of provision of primary-level education services from 10.6 per cent to 20.3 per cent[13]
- Projected number of pupils in partly government-aided schools: 0[14]
- Total number of pupils in government-aided schools: 5,634,614
- Total number of teachers on government payroll: 114,530 (of which only 274 are untrained)
- Average teacher remuneration per annum excluding premium in Local Currency Units (LCU): 1,884,277
- Total teacher remuneration excluding premium (millions of LCU): 215,807 million
- Total teacher remuneration including premium (millions of LCU): 218,272 million
- Spending on inputs other than teachers (millions of LCU): 103,890 million
- Total expenditure on inputs other than teachers as a percentage of total recurrent spending: 32.2 per cent
- Projected total off-budget recurrent spending on primary education (millions of LCU): 459, 640 million[15]

Background to continued 'mushrooming' of private schools

The principal components of the UPE policy were the elimination of tuition fees and Parent Teacher Association (PTA) fees for the vast majority of pupils. This resulted in an unexpectedly massive increase in enrolments (see figure below). Since that landmark declaration, enrolments in primary education have jumped from 2.7 million in 1996 to approximately 7.2 million in 2002, moving Uganda much closer to achieving UPE.

However, the sudden and dramatic expansion of enrolments has put tremendous strain on the entire education system in Uganda, most specifically on the quality of education. This is partly reflected in the deterioration in academic performance of pupils. The deterioration in the quality of education has been blamed on overcrowding in government-aided primary schools and delays in paying teachers.

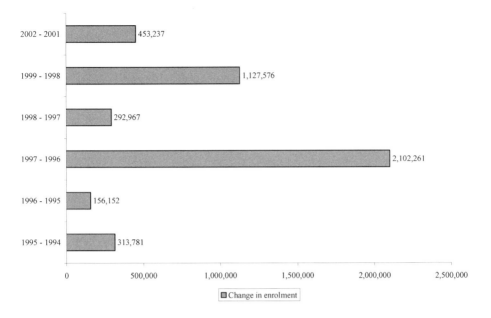

2002 - 2001		453,237
1999 - 1998		1,127,576
1998 - 1997		292,967
1997 - 1996		2,102,261
1996 - 1995		156,152
1995 - 1994		313,781

☐ Change in enrolment

Figure 6.1 Change in national enrolment figures, 1994–2002
Source: UNESCO (2000) EFA Assessment 2000 Country Report for Uganda

The increase in enrolment in government primary schools with no commensurate increase in the number of teachers (actually made worse by a ban on teacher recruitment from 2003–2006) led to teacher-pupil ratios getting significantly worse. This saw teachers unable to effectively teach, or to assess or monitor the academic performance of pupils. Interviews with parents and education officers further highlighted the effects of decreasing education quality in government schools on the mushrooming of privately-owned schools. A case in point is in Gulu Municipality, where at least three privately-owned primary schools (Mother Angioletta, Bright Valley and Labour-Line Primary School) have been registered and about eight others licensed to operate since the start of UPE.

Definitions of different forms of schools in Uganda

In Uganda, a school's status of operation is determined by who runs it. This could be different from the founding body (government, religious, parents, entrepreneurs or others) and the funding source. In essence, this relates to the authority that has the biggest stake in the school management. There are several forms of non-government schools in Uganda, but the Uganda Education Bill (2002) categorises education institutions into three categories:

• Public education institutions/government-founded institutions

- Government grant-aided education institutions (also referred to as community schools)

- Private institutions, which include both local and international

While the Bill outlines the three broad education provisions, the different categories of private school are not articulated.[16] As a result, some community schools are categorised as private schools. The Uganda Education Bill (2002) defines a private school as one that 'is not founded by government and receiving no statutory grants from government'. The growth of private schools has its roots in the policy on democratisation of education (Republic of Uganda, 1992) and the liberalisation and privatisation policy implemented as part of the World Bank and IMF Structural Adjustment Policies from 1986. Liberalisation of the economy meant that private investors could provide services like health, education and transport to citizens. In the education sector, it led to the proliferation of privately-owned schools, especially in urban and peri-urban areas.

In some cases, the lack of nearby government schools led to the growth of low-cost private schools. This phenomenon was fed by the fact that the supply of newly-trained teachers was too great to be absorbed by government schools. The government ban on recruitment of teachers that lasted nearly three years from 2003 and only lifted in 2006, demonstrates the low-absorption capacity. These teachers tend to start up low-cost schools in an effort to create employment. By 2006, there were 150,120 schoolteachers in all primary schools and most of them (64 per cent) were grade 3[17] trained with a 59:41 ratio of male to female teachers.[18]

In an interview, one respondent described the formation of private schools thus:

'Private schools' proprietors come together to invest in education. In terms of management, ownership is private; when two or three people are together, they are called a Board of Directors (BOD), mobilise resources and invest in a school. The BOD then nominates a School Management Committee and a Parent Teacher Association (PTA).'[19]

Private schools are started by individuals or institutions to provide education services, but with an objective to make a profit; they do not receive any public funding.[20]

The Education Bill defines government-founded schools as 'public schools or schools founded by government.' A government grant-aided school is one that is not founded by government, but receives statutory grants in form of aid from government and is jointly managed by the foundation body and government. The grants received include annual recurrent and capitation grants from government, salaries and wages, and instructional materials to cover operational costs. Such schools do not depend entirely on government grants, but receive some public funding. Universal Primary Education is described in the Bill as a programme with free education, where obstacles to accessing primary education have been removed. UPE is the provision of primary education to all children of school-going age.

Apart from the definitions provided by the Education Bill (2002), *community schools* in Uganda are generally started by rural communities as 'self-help initiatives' in areas where the nearest school is more than two kilometres away. They usually start under temporary structures (reeds, mud and wattle or sometimes just poles with a tin roof), or sheltered in existing community structures such as churches, and sometimes simply located in a compound with classes held under trees. Up to a point when government expresses interest to take over ownership and management, these schools receive limited subsidies and funding from government. Such funding might include, for example, roofing an incomplete classroom block constructed by community members, posting teachers to the school and providing a few teaching resources. Ownership of these schools is usually transferred to government at the earliest opportunity. Although community schools do not have a profit-making objective, they are sometimes categorised as private education institutions.[21]

Religious affiliated private schools

These are owned and run by religious bodies that in Uganda include the Catholic Church, Church of Uganda, Seventh Day Adventists and Muslims or 'developed from religious missions'.[22] They may be supported externally by parent bodies with the same religious affiliation. Usually they also require the parents to contribute a small fee towards the running of the school. However, owing to the history of education having an inclination to religion, government now has a significant control over a huge majority of religious schools through recruitment and remuneration of teachers, providing curriculum and subsidising teaching and learning resources, offering supervision services, accrediting and providing registration. The role of religious bodies remains in governance; at least a quarter of the school's Board of Governors are representatives of the religious body.

Low-cost private schools

A low-cost private school is a non-government school owned by an individual or individuals with relatively affordable fees in relation to its locality. The fee is seen as affordable (ranging from 15,000 local currency units [LCU; approximately £5] to 28,000 LCU [approximately £9] per school term).[23] Low-cost private schools are usually in peri-urban areas and are usually within 1–2km of a government school.

High-cost private schools

Like the low-cost private schools, high-cost private schools are owned by an individual or individuals and include international schools. They usually include boarding sections and are associated with high fees and assured high-quality services. Clientele for high-cost private schools are usually upper- and middle-class citizens. Often due to high motivation of teachers and good teaching and learning resources, these schools have a 'good academic reputation'. These private schools are often located in urban areas, particularly in the central region of Uganda.

The government's responsibilities

The responsibility of government in private education institutions, as enshrined in the Education Bill (2002), is to ensure that private institutions conform to government rules and regulations governing the provision of education services in the country. The Bill also lays out procedures for government aiding education institutions: '...any education institution to qualify for grant-aiding shall have fulfilled all the regulations for licensing and registration'. Government, at its discretion, determines which applications received from founder bodies are considered for grant-aid. Responsibility of government in state and grant-aided education institutions includes: ensuring that trained teachers are deployed; paying salaries and allowances to teachers; paying salaries and wages to established non-teaching staff; paying all statutory grants; appointing heads of these institutions in consultation with the foundation bodies; providing educational materials and other capital development inputs; and providing national pupil admission guidelines. The Education Bill states, 'no person shall teach in any public or private school of any description unless (s)he is registered as a teacher or licensed to teach under this Bill.' Only those persons who successfully complete a teacher-training course are entitled, on application to the Director of Education, to be registered as teachers.

In the event that a government-aided school wishes to revert to private institution status, the government regulations governing school charges and admissions will apply for a period not exceeding four years to allow for pupils/students admitted to it to complete their cycle or find alternative institutions. Government recovers 70 per cent of the value of public funding towards the development of physical facilities from the foundation body (recovered in phases over a maximum period of ten years) from the institution that wishes to revert to private status.

Methodology

In investigating the impact of the low-cost private sector education on achieving Universal Primary Education in Uganda, this study was limited to 'private-sector, low-fee paying schools owned by an individual or individuals or other form of commercial enterprise.' Schools founded by communities and religious bodies, and international and high-fee private schools were excluded.

Research processes

The study was composed of four main processes for data gathering:

- A review of available surveys and EMIS data;

- A review of secondary data and prior studies carried out on private education in Uganda and developing countries with similar characteristics to Uganda;

- Key informant interviews, which included education administrators, District Inspectors of Schools (DIS), District Education Officers from the Lira and Mityana districts and a proprietor of a private school; and

- A detailed study of two selected schools.

With guidance from the Lira District Inspector of Schools, two schools, a government-aided and a low-cost private school, were selected in the same parish in Lira district in Northern Uganda.[24] The district is neither very rural nor very urban; it has characteristics of a typical district having a blend of urban, peri-urban and rural areas. The selected schools and the school communities had attributes that are common to peri-urban environments such as payment of school fees by cash, topped up with payments in kind. This is typical of peri-urban communities, where small business thrives alongside subsistence farming, often of very small pieces of land.

Case studies were developed of the two schools, based on interviews with school proprietors, head teachers, pupils, parents and opinion leaders from each community. Schoolteachers helped in selecting the children and parents to be interviewed. A total of four children and four parents were deliberately selected from middle-income and poor households to be interviewed. The pupils were selected from the middle and upper classes[25] (11–12 years old) for credible responses.

Limitations

Field visits were limited due to budget constraints. Private schools have very weak documentation and record-keeping processes. Frequent power interruptions also constrained receipt of data from education offices and affected analysis and report writing.

Findings

Education statistics

In 1999, the Ministry of Education and Sports (MoES) embarked on developing an Education Management Information System (EMIS) to improve timeliness, accuracy, reliability and availability of information to various users. While the design showed that the district would be the focal point of the system, **decentralisation of data processing in the EMIS had not yet taken off at the time of writing despite numerous efforts ... because of infrastructural constraints. However, a lot has been achieved in terms of data gathering;**[26] the information in the database enables trend-analysis by time or by location, producing summarised statistical details at the national and district levels, or full details at sub-county, parish or school levels collected annually with the following range of information:

- Key education ratios: teacher: pupil; classroom: pupil; and textbook: pupil

- Gross and net enrolment and intake rates

- Repeaters, dropouts, the disabled and orphans

- Teachers' professional and academic qualifications

- School infrastructure, school finances etc.[27]

The advent of EMIS at district and national level has seen an improvement in primary school data capture. Data collection is carried out at district level and consolidated at national level. Statistical abstracts and reports generated by EMIS contain detailed statistics on profiles of education indices, usually presented in three broad categories: government schools, private education provisions and community schools. It is worthy of mention, however, that disaggregation of private education provisions in these reports is seldom made. In addition, comparison of data at national, district and school level on private schools sometimes shows significant differences.

This begs several questions: are all private schools aware of the requirement to provide data to the respective district education offices? Are the data requirements and the attendant data instruments accessible and well articulated to private education managers? Do private schools co-operate adequately in provision of required data? Could it be that a significant proportion of the information collected on private schools is inadequate or unreliable for analysis and subsequent publishing?

It is evident that data capture of non-government education provisions is very thinly captured. Data on many parameters pertaining to several private education provisions is not reflected in the overall national education statistics. In addition, government records only capture data of officially-registered private schools. This data is not presented in a way that shows the status of different types of private schooling. Furthermore, ambiguity in descriptions of different categories of private education provisions has resulted in some community schools being classified as private while others are categorised as public schools.

Tables 6.1 and 6.2, below, show some of the data that is captured at MoES and by district in the EMIS.

It is evident from the tables that efforts are made to collect data on private education provision. However, as remarked by one of the education officials in the district,

Table 6.1 Primary school enrolment patterns in Lira district[28]

	Lower		Middle		Upper		Total	
	Boys	Girls	Boys	Girls	Boys	Girls	Boys	Girls
Government enrolment	39,480	36,721	21,432	18,058	14,039	10,140	75,236	65,083
	52%	48%	54%	46%	58%	42%	54%	46%
Private enrolment	Data in absolute terms is missing							
	58%	42%	67%	33%	65%	35%	63%	37%

'...sometimes due to late submission of data, unreliable, incomplete or missing data, estimates are used when it comes to reporting data on private schools.' The fact that relative values are given in the table, while the absolute values are missing, suggests that estimates are being used. It is also widely acknowledged that data on private education provision captured in government information systems is either absent, partial or incorrect.

Flaws in data collection, capture and reporting

There are caveats and limitations to primary and secondary data presented in the EMIS. For example, the data presented does not reflect the total schools' population, but is rather from schools where responses were received. The table below shows response rates by sub-sector.[29]

Worth noting is the fact that there was an increase in the number of private primary schools between the year 2005 and 2006 from 11.1 per cent of the total number of primary schools to 13.3 per cent, while the percentage of government primary schools dropped from 83.3 per cent to 80.9 per cent in the same period.

Of the total number of primary schools that responded shown in Table 6.2 above (statistics not disaggregated by ownership of school), 6.4 per cent are situated in urban areas, 11.9 per cent in peri-urban areas and 78.5 per cent are located in rural areas. The location of 3.3 per cent of the schools was not stated. In addition, 82.7 per cent of the total 14,385 were registered, 4.7 per cent licensed (whereby the school is not fully officially registered, but has a licence to operate), 7.9 per cent were not registered, while the registration status of 674 primary schools (4.7 per cent) was not known.[31]

One caveat of using the tables in the abstract is that they present subsets of schools; combining these subsets will not necessarily give the totals shown in the summary table due to incidence of unknown values. For example, combining the tables showing enrolment in government-, private- and community-owned schools does not give the total enrolment. This is because some schools did not provide information about their ownership, hence are not included in the summary table.[32]

Furthermore, the current EMIS in Uganda has limitations with regard to data collection at three levels, namely, at schools, at district level and at MoES headquarters.

Table 6.2 Response rates by sub-sector

	No. of schools in database	No. that responded	Response rate	Enrolment in 2006
Government	11,883	11,643	98%	6,668,931
Private	4,806	1,877	39%	476,215
Community	1,118	865[30]	77%	211,924
Total	17,807	14,385	81%	7,362,938

'Enrolment figures tend to be over-estimated, leading to a NER greater than 100 per cent. Some schools and districts declare higher enrolment to attract higher UPE capitation since the disbursements to schools are determined by the number of pupils reported. This criterion is ranked high on the list of factors for inflated enrolment figures among some schools.'[33] Private schools have also been accused of irregular reporting and submitting incomplete and flawed data.[34]

Irregularities in reporting on private education provision

The phenomenon described above is reflected in different EMIS cross-tabulation tables where responses – at best – show 'all primary schools inclusive of private and community ownership'.

In Table 6.3, below, private providers and community schools are classified under one category. The absence of a detailed breakdown of the contributions by the different non-government educations suggests several hypotheses: that probably the contribution of individual categories is too small, hence the need to 'collapse' the different categories into one category during data presentation; or that inadequate

Table 6.3 Trends in key education indicators

Key education indicators	Year 2000		Year 2001		Overall comments	
	All schools	Only gov't schools	All schools	Only gov't schools	All schools	Only gov't schools
Pupils	6,559,013	5,351,099	6,900,916	5,917,216	5% growth	11% growth
Teachers	110,366	82,148	127,038	101,818	15% growth	24% growth
Classrooms	68,523	50,370	77,200	60,199	13% growth	19.5% growth
Pupil-teacher ratio	59	65	54	58	8.5% improvement	Up by 7 pts
Pupil-classroom ratio	96	106	89	98	7.2% improvement	Up by 8 pts
Pupil-textbook ratio – lower primary	6	5	5	5	16% improvement	No change
Pupil-textbook ratio – upper primary	3	3	3	3	No change	No change
Net enrolment in P7	10%	8%	10%	9.8%	No change	1.8% improvement

Source: MoES (2002b) and MoES (2001) Education Sector Fact File

information is collected/received from non-government providers and hence aggregate estimates are used.

However, further analysis of the table negates the first hypothesis; both the absolute contributions in discrete years and the contributions in the relative changes between the two time series strongly indicate a significant contribution of non-government education providers. A proportion of 18 per cent and 26 per cent in enrolment and teacher numbers respectively contributed by non-government education providers in 2000 is by no means small, although the contributions drop to 14 per cent and 20 per cent respectively in the following year. It is also evident that the contribution of non-government providers towards pupil-classroom ratios is much lower as reflected in the low ratios, and further in the relative growth of 13 per cent overall compared to 19.5 per cent for 'only government' schools between the two years.

The District Inspector of Schools of Lira District suggested the reason for the under-reporting of private provision in the district included the under-resourcing of the department responsible for data collection: 'Sometimes data is collected from private schools, but because of inadequate manpower, it is not entered in the EMIS... Secondly, data is not collected as regularly as it should be on a termly [three-month] basis due to limited personnel, the distance between schools and logistical limitations, especially transport to cover all the schools in the district...' This suggests that education officials prioritise which sites to visit so as to use the meagre resources available to them to collect data from public schools.

Omission of private sector contributions in many national records and reports on primary school education is partly explained by unavailability of data on private schools. It is *alleged* that this data is 'not readily available and always inadequate for detailed analysis.' As one of the District Education Officials in Lira District remarked, 'many of the private school owners *disappear* from their schools every time the District Education Department visits to collect data...' It is widely believed by education officials that private school owners relate the data collection exercise to taxation and hence do everything possible to avoid providing the required information. Meanwhile, owners and managers of private schools argue that they submit data on their schools to the district as stipulated, but that it is rarely or incorrectly captured in the district databases, as revealed in the quote below:

> 'We provide monthly returns to the District Education Office, and this information includes the number of pupils, the number of teachers, records on utilities like desks, financial accountability... The district keeps these records although their reports do not always show correct information about us.'
> *Source*: Deputy headmistress of Canon Lawrence Demonstration Primary School (a government school)

Another hypothesis to explain the under-reporting of private schools is the long and bureaucratic registration process of private schools. The long list of minimum requirements, as was noted by the director of one of the private schools that participated in this study, is not a major challenge: 'the uphill task has to do with the actual registration process', which is described as 'a painfully slow bureaucratic process.' There are no exceptions for low-cost private schools in the registration process; all private schools are required to meet the government standard.[35] In addition, the compulsory requirement for private schools to operate as 'provisional schools for a minimum of two years,' before rigorous assessment for registration partly explains the omissions in data collection, as priority may be given to registered private education providers. These schools are usually far fewer in number and of the high-cost variety. The challenges experienced by private schools during the registration process, form a major source of explanation for the relatively few registered private schools in Uganda compared to the total numbers in existence.

Contradictions in statistical reporting on private education

Tables 6.4 and 6.5 demonstrate the disparities in statistics between the MoES and district EMIS data. While it would be expected that the MoES data be compiled from the individual district databases, it is evident that this is not the case in the two data sets (note disparities in discrete and aggregate values). This throws the accuracy and completeness of the data into doubt. It is certain that there are more private education providers in existence than are represented here in the data.

Table 6.4 Number of primary schools by ownership and by district – as compiled by MoES

District	Government	Community	Private
Adjumani	68	14	2
Apac	284	2	
Arua	311	36	
Gulu	232		5
Kaberamaido	85	3	0
Katakwi	169	4	
Kitgum	169	0	6
Kotido	104	0	0
Kumi	220	3	4
Lira	332		10
Moroto	45	8	
Moyo	74		3
Nakapiripirit	40	15	0
Nebbi	220	8	1
Pader	182	35	2
Pallisa	186		
Soroti	151	19	1
Yumbe	113	5	0
Total	2,985	152	34

Table 6.5 Number of primary schools by ownership and by district – as compiled by districts

District	Government	Community	Private	Total
Adjumani	57	23	4	84
Apac	267	10	2	279
Arua	300	31	26	357
Gulu	219	3	7	229
Kaberamaido	0	0	0	0
Katakwi	0	0	0	0
Kitgum	130	25	6	161
Kotido	0	0	0	0
Kumi	198	22	3	223
Lira	314	9	8	331
Moroto	39	6	0	45
Moyo	61	11	4	76
Nakapiripit	0	0	0	0
Nebbi	0	0	0	0
Pader	179	26	5	210
Pallisa	183	6	11	200
Soroti	154	22	5	181
Yumbe	80	21	9	110
Total	2,181	215	90	2,486

The public/private choice

The choice of public or private school is largely made at the family level. The Uganda DHS EdData Survey (UDES) revealed, for instance, that in rural areas fathers are more likely than in urban areas to make the decision on whether a child should attend school at all – and therefore about what sort of school he/she will attend. In Northern Uganda, a region that has been hit by civil war for the last two decades, fathers are more likely than in other regions to make the final decisions. The table below illustrates decision-making about school attendance.

Table 6.6 Who decides about school attendance[36]

Percentage distribution of parents/guardians by which household member decides whether children attend school, according to background characteristics.											
Background characteristic	Household member making final decision									Total	Number of parents/ guardians
	Mother	Father	Both parents	Guardians	Child	Parent/ guardian with child	Someone else	Decision not made	Don't know/ missing		
Residence											
Urban	24.7	26.5	29.4	12.4	0.3	4.8	0.1	0.7	1.1	100	481
Rural	16.5	39.9	26	10.9	0.2	4.7	0.2	1	0.5	100	3,765
Region											
Central	23.3	29	25.1	11.9	0.1	8.3	0.2	1.5	0.5	100	1,409
Eastern	10	44	28.5	12.9	0.2	3	0.3	0.4	0.7	100	1,164
Northern	15.6	55.9	18.9	6.7	0.2	1.7	0.3	0	0.6	100	646
Western	19.1	33.9	30.7	10.4	0.2	3.6	0.1	1.6	0.4	100	1,026
Total	17.5	38.4	26.4	11	0.2	4.7	0.2	1	0.6	100	4,246

Possible reasons for choice of school

There are a host of factors that parents, guardians and/or children consider in making a decision on which type of school the child should attend. Some of these factors are directly related to school provisions, while others pertain largely to the socio-economic conditions of the family.

The reason parents choose to send their children to private schools can be summed up as dissatisfaction with UPE. UPE has been criticised for the following reasons:

'Children made to study for free, but UPE is spoilt by the high number of children, limited classrooms, and poor pupil-teacher relationships.'

'Parents have left everything to government; parents no longer mind about children's performance, as promotion to the next class is "automatic," because they don't pay tuition fees.'

The policy of automatic promotion has been highly criticised because parents feel children are promoted to the next class even when they are not ready; at the end of the seven-year primary school cycle, some children have not mastered basic literacy and numeracy, because of poor-quality education.

'UPE has generally been more of a failure than a success – most pupils who study in UPE schools from P1 to P7 usually fail the primary level examination (PLE).'

'UPE policies are spoiling children, for example caning children was abolished; children must be punished for any wrong-doing to make them learn from their mistakes – inappropriate outside practices [children's rights] are spoiling our children – both in school performance and discipline! Discipline in schools is often associated with good performance and therefore a brighter future for the children by parents ... this cannot be said of UPE schools.'
Source: Interview with private schoolteacher

Table 6.7 Explicit and implicit costs incurred in public and private schools

Costs incurred	
Private school	Government school
School fees	PTA fees
Water bill	Development fund (about 7,000 shillings per
Food; beans and maize meal	school term)
Medical fee	Brooms
Fee for latrine maintenance	Costs for porridge for lunch (usually 2-5kg
Development fee	maize seeds)
School uniform (in some schools this is	School uniform
optional)	

Low-cost Private Education

One could argue that UPE in Uganda is not free, as it has some explicit and implicit costs. Such costs, varying from one situation to another, may include uniform costs, scholastic materials, building and development fees, food and other non-financial school requirements such as brooms and firewood. Putting this into context, on average, a typical rural household in Uganda in 2000 spent USh26,870 (£9) on public schooling or USh128,160 (£42) on private schooling on various school costs during the year. The mean average expenditures on schooling among pupils attending public schools was about one-fifth the mean average for pupils attending non-public schools. In the past, private education was considered expensive and only served the middle class in urban areas, not the poor. However, with the growth of low-cost private schools, this perception is slowly changing. With the low cost of hiring teachers in rural private schools, these schools allow savings to be passed on to parents through low fees. Why then do parents still pay for the relatively expensive private schools? A probable reason could be inferred from the response of one 68-year-old, Joyce Auma, of Lira on why she continues to send her grandchild to a low-cost private school:

> 'If there is poor quality meat sold at USh1,000 a kilo and in the neighbouring market stall there is better meat sold at USh3,000 a kilo, I would rather take the latter even if I will just have it for once and take ages without having meat again!'

Academic performance and level of pupil engagement

While government strives to provide equal access to quality education through the UPE programme, a dominant public view in Uganda is that government primary schools offer varying standards of education judged by their performance on the national public primary leaving examination (PLE). One possible reason for this variety is the policy of automatic promotion from one class to another. It is widely acknowledged that many children do not attend classes regularly, do not concentrate in class and only come to sit the end-of-term or end-of-year exams, as this is all that is required for transition to the next class. However, after completion of the seven years primary school cycle, there are substantial numbers of pupils who fail the PLE, which is the prerequisite for entrance into secondary school.

A review of statistical information on primary education in Mityana district reveals that the average academic performance of private schools is better than that of government schools – especially in mathematics. Some of the explanations provided included the fact that in private schools there is no automatic promotion, which *ensures* quality; and that remedial classes are offered, especially to slow learners, to help pupils learn faster and catch up with others. It was also stated that the relatively small number of children in private school classes makes it possible to ensure good discipline among the children, which is a key factor linked to academic performance. Good discipline is far less likely to be achieved in UPE schools, where the number of children is large, posing a challenge to teachers to control the class; large numbers also hamper effective teaching and learning.

'Two girls joined our school from a UPE school in primary 6; we could not keep one of them here because she could not read words in English! Yet a primary 3 child here could read a whole sentence! And not only that, she was also very rude when answering teachers.'
Source: Teacher at Gallary Junior School Mukono, Uganda

'It is not enough to get children into schools and retain them there. What matters is how effectively they are being educated and how effectively resources are being used to promote learning.'
Source: Teacher in Mityana

Teacher absenteeism is one indicator of poor efficiency. On average, about 19 per cent of teachers were absent from their school on days when they should be working during the UDES survey. Anecdotal evidence indicates that the rate of teacher presence in class (as reported by pupils to their parents) has a strong correlation to the decision on which school the child should attend. Private schools offer better performance on at least some key measures of school quality.

'One teacher who did not even have [teaching] qualifications, but was very committed to his job was followed by parents wherever he went [whichever school he taught in]'
Source: Parent

Rogers and his co-authors (Kremer, 2004) find that in India, teacher absence is one-third lower in private than in public schools. There is more regular and rigorous supervision of both the teachers and children in the private school by the head teacher and the proprietors of the school, since there is an element of having to make a profit. Consequently, teachers demonstrate more responsibility and commitment in private schools.

It is worth noting that district-level inspectors and Centre Co-ordinating Tutors usually visit all recognised/registered schools two or three times a term, spending barely 20 minutes in each class they visit. This is due to logistical impediments and the long distances between the many schools assigned to them. Face-to-face interactions between the supervisor and the teacher in public schools are very rare.

School facilities

The data below suggests that government schools are overall slightly better resourced in terms of infrastructure, especially in sanitation facilities, compared to private schools.[37] It is noteworthy that urban government schools have more infrastructure than the average government and private school. In view of the fact that more people are choosing to send their children to private school, it seems that private schools are making up for this lack of infrastructure with dedicated and hardworking staff, and an average teacher-pupil ratio of 1:35. This enables teachers to give adequate

Table 6.8 Primary school facilities in Lira District, 2007

Facilities	Averages			Case study schools	
	Government	Private	Urban govt	Canon Lawrence (govt)	Cornerstone (Private)
Classrooms	8	12	12	25	14
Infant classrooms	7	0	3	4	0
Total	15	12	15	29	14
Library	0	2	0	0	1
Store	1	1	1	1	0
Offices	2	3	1	3	0
Staffroom	1	1	0	0	0
Teachers	7	8	11	16	9
Girls' latrines	9	7	16	16	3
Boys' latrines	9	6	13	15	2
Total	18	13	29	31	5
Teachers' houses	3	2	4	2	1
Desks	168	152	185	114	197

attention to each child and hence improve the effectiveness of instruction and quality of learning.

Level of parental involvement in children's education

Parents' involvement in school issues makes a school better according to the Uganda DHS EdData Survey 2001. Parents' contribution in public schools is mostly material, rather than their providing views and ideas. Unlike in the government schools, parents find it easier to contribute their views in private schools and these are then implemented. The survey further asserts that paying fees makes private schools more accountable to parents.

Threats That Private Schools Present to Government Schools

The threats that private schools present to government schools, as summed up by one district education officer:

- Private schools are more popular in terms of academic performance;
- Government schools tend to be more relaxed in terms of morality and discipline; private schools are stricter;
- The number of private schools is increasing every year, which is a threat to enrolments in government schools; and
- 'All informed parents are now investing in education by sending their children to private schools.'

Recommendations

Current and potential roles of government in private school provision

In Uganda, overall enrolment of children of school-going age (6–12) stands at 84 per cent; overall enrolment shot up from 2m in 1996 just before the advent of Universal Primary Education (UPE) to about 7.3m in 2003. Even with these tremendous increases in school enrolments, the government has acknowledged the need for non-state education provision. One of the recommendations mentioned by interview participants was that government should provide an enabling environment for private schools, as this will contribute to achieving 'Education for All' (EFA).

One of the important roles of the state in private education is regulation to ensure the quality of education. Regulation could include ensuring the adequacy of financial resources and learning and teaching facilities, ensuring that content taught conforms to the recommended primary school national curriculum and ensuring that teaching staff are all qualified. This calls for the increased and active involvement of the state in financing, supervising and providing continuous professional development of teachers for quality education provision. The initiative of funding private schools that charged less than USh10,000 per term during the first four years of implementing UPE may be invaluable if it can be reviewed and structured in line with the unique target groups of pupils and the environments in which the private schools operate.

Furthermore, earmarking funds for low-cost private primary schools in the Medium-Term Budget Framework (MTBF) and the three-year national, district and lower local government development plans may pay dividends. In recognition of the role that low-cost private primary schools in Uganda are making towards achievement of the education MDGs, financial support to ease bottlenecks – especially in terms of meeting the remuneration costs of teachers – would probably see private schools play a more significant and effective role in education access and quality provision. Lessons on such funding modalities could be drawn from the health sector, where some private health provision is funded under the government financing mechanism.

The involvement of government may also include providing teaching and learning materials, or at least providing subsidies on teaching and learning resources or tax exemptions on capital investments, such as building costs made by private schools.

In-service support should be provided to teachers in private schools through continuous professional development (CPD) by the Centre Co-ordination Tutors (CCTs). Supervision visits by CCTs and District Inspectors of Schools should be strengthened in private schools. Alongside the ongoing teacher-development courses, it would be useful for private schoolteachers to be involved in one-off or periodic teacher training events, such as in the PIASCY programme.

Uganda: study materials

Comparison of government and private case study schools

	Government (Grade I)	Private[38] (Grade I)
Teachers' training, qualifications, support received and daily roles	22 teachers: 10 female and 12 male All teachers are grade 3 or grade 5 by training (it's a requirement that all teachers must be qualified, i.e. must hold at least a grade 3 certificate) Some grade 3 teachers have been enrolled on the continuous professional development courses (CPDs), conducted by Centre Co-ordinating Tutors (CCTs) through core Primary Teachers Colleges (PTCs) At least once a month, supervision visits by CCTs and school inspectors, especially in classes with teachers on CPD Refresher courses for teachers are held regularly and all teachers are entitled to attend There are opportunities for up-grading qualifications through CPD Teaching resources are received from the Ministry of Education and Sports (MoES) through the CCT. They also receive subsidies for textbooks by applying to central government (MoES) through the official textbook supplier All teachers are expected to strictly adhere to government standards, e.g. teachers' code of conduct in exhibiting professionalism In-school supervisory measures conducted through assessment and approval of teachers' schemes of work	About 70 per cent of teachers possess at least grade 3 certificate, and 30 per cent are untrained There is no systematic training or refresher training organised for teachers and no supervision visits from school inspectors Typical day for P4-P7:[39] 8:30–10:30 Classes 10:30–11:00 Break time 11: 00–1:00 Classes 1:00–2:00 Lunch break 2: 00–3:50 Free, but guided, pupils' activities 3:50–4:00 Giving homework All pupils P4-P7 have homework everyday; P1–P3 lessons end at 3pm Quality assurance realised through: • Assessment of teachers by head teacher, e.g. sitting in class, ensuring that homework is given and all books marked, jointly preparing schemes of work and a few lesson plans • Implementation of schemes of work and thorough lesson planning • Ensuring teachers have textbooks • Refresher training for teachers organised by CCT at various centres (only a few teachers benefit) 'The only supervisory support received from government is inspection of school activities – mainly to give conditions on number of teachers, desks, construction of toilets etc.'

Children's school attendance	Average attendance for lower classes is more erratic than for middle and higher classes. Average attendance rates are placed at 76 per cent, 82 per cent and 84 per cent in the three levels respectively, with minimal variations between boys and girls	Average Attendance is 95 per cent – boys more absent than girls, as their parents will keep them away from school more for labour
Teachers' remuneration and other incentives	Minimum gross salary is USh 120,000 per month. The pay varies – but average is USh200,000. This is paid monthly – even during school holidays – and there is an annual salary increment of 21,000; teachers are entitled to gratuity payments	Salary level depends on length of employment at school A new teacher earns USh80,000 per month; after one term, pay increases to USh100,000. Maximum pay is USh150,000
	Other benefits Teachers are entitled to lunch and a break for tea	**Other benefits** Free breakfast and free lunch Free education in the school for one child of each teacher
	The biggest single expenditure is teachers' salaries, which takes up nearly 65 per cent of a school's total budget (source: Interviews with head teacher/proprietor of private school in Mbale)	Free house/accommodation; a large plot of land where teachers can farm *Note*: Teachers are not paid during school holidays, hence they receive salary for about nine months in a calendar year
Class – dynamics	Average teacher-pupil ratio is 1:70 for lower classes; 1:91 for middle classes; and 1:50 for upper classes. Teachers follow a new curriculum: this is thematic for P1–P3, transitional for P4 and subject-based for P5–P7 Strict adherence to policy on mother tongue – although with difficulty	Average teacher pupil ratio 1:35 Children are more active and engaged – teacher in a better position to provide support to each child; discipline ensured through relatively low teacher-pupil ratio Transition from one class to another is not automatic; a minimum of 200 marks (50 per cent) in all the four subjects is a prerequisite. This calls for more academic effort on the part of teachers and pupils Language of instruction for all classes is English (contrary to government policy).[40] However, the government's old syllabus and curriculum are used

Challenges faced by teachers	'Unstable school curriculum' – which is frequently reviewed and changed	Teaching lower classes in local language is very difficult because children in nursery school are taught in English. In addition, teaching materials in local language are scarce and technical support is inadequate
	Abrupt policy changes in education, such as policy on language of instruction, caning and promotion of children from one class to another	
		The teaching and learning materials, which are provided by the school, are limited, e.g. textbooks, mathematical instruments etc.
	Meagre salaries – 'I am being underpaid! Only USh180,000/= per month!'; late salary payments	
	Undisciplined pupils – the large number of pupils makes it difficult to ensure discipline	Workload is heavy because teachers are few. This is aggravated by 'little payment, which cannot cater for all the basic personal needs. In addition, because our directors are also teachers, if their salaries are delayed, so are ours.'
		Lack of classrooms, a library or chalkboards
		Opportunities for capacity building by CCTs and further studies in institutions are not provided; extra-curricular activities like debates and networking among others are not facilitated, making participation in competition difficult
Challenges faced by parents		'Schools fees are a challenge, but usually we talk to the school authorities to allow a grace period'
		Price-fluctuations of essential goods e.g. sugar, soap etc. is expensive for parents
		Buying foodstuff, e.g. *posho* and beans
		Other expenses, e.g. medical fees every term, even if a child doesn't fall sick
		Buying a ready-made school uniform from the school, and scholastic materials
Extra-curricula activities	Sports, music, dance and drama (MDD) – government schools send pupils for competitions, thus helping to make pupils more confident	Sports and MDD are mainly organised by district education officials, and sometimes private schools are not considered for competitions. In particular, there is seldom financial support for private schools to participate, especially at district or higher levels

Interview notes from Uganda study

Interviews with District Inspector of Schools and two teachers on government versus private schools

	Government schools	Private schools
Strengths	Parents enjoy benefit of government aid e.g. payment of teachers' salaries, grants to run school activities	Focus on performance by both teachers and pupils.
	Schools are led by the rules and regulations of government	Administrator is the sole overseer, so it is easier to plan and easily identify weakness and make necessary correction. No bureaucracy
	Teachers are protected by government acts, e.g. salary payments and retirement benefits	Community schools which remain private tend to consider the role of the community in management decisions
	Schools are open to frequent inspections and to government support, e.g. during times of disaster	
	More secure finance (grants for UPE)	Private schools tend to perform better academically than UPE schools
	Good infrastructure – classrooms, teachers' houses and administration blocks. Large land plots for expansion	Private schools instil more discipline in children; they do not adhere to some stringent government policies like not caning children
	Teachers have better pay (on the government scale). Food for teachers is sometimes better and teachers have opportunities to access capacity building initiatives, joint conferences etc. Incentives are given for marking papers, attending workshops etc.	Parents are more responsive to demands made by private schools, e.g. provision of textbooks for children
		There is an almost nil dropout rate, because parents have had to pay school fees; they thus force their children to study hard and remain in school
	Teachers have access to loans, and their workload is lighter. They have good opportunities for professional development and good job security. Teachers in government schools are pensionable, enjoy gratuities and have access to further studies.	Demands levied on schools by parents of private schools are much more focused on improving performance of pupils
	Teachers enjoy freedom of speech.	Talent development is high and there is strong support from parents

		towards the development of the school, especially through the PTA
	They are also better in other extra curricular activities because they have better facilities.	Good time management
		There are minimal complaints from parents, because payments made by parents are invested in the administration of the school
		Good welfare for pupils, teachers and support staff
Weaknesses	Bureaucracy, e.g. in disciplining teachers, gives room to laissez-faire type of administration	Meetings are infrequent, thus power tends to be abused; no freedom of expression for teachers
	Massive recruitment has meant 'hiring ineffective and rotten teachers'	Sometimes parents are taken for granted, their views are not considered
	Transition and dropout rates are very high because of free service	

Teachers' views on why people send their children to private school

Why do you think parents choose to send their children to private school?
• Teachers are very hardworking, active and punctual for lessons
• Pupils are more disciplined and smarter
• Owing to extra academic effort by teachers and pupils, the syllabus is completed early and adequate time is made for revision
• Adequate teacher-pupil ratio, average 1:35
• If a child doesn't know how to read and write, they are given special attention and made to learn fast; because pupils are few per class, it is thus easier to treat each child individually
• Efficiency and quality
• 'In second term alone, we received 30 pupils from neighbouring UPE schools – due to better performance of pupils and speak good English' [sic]
• 'Poor performance by UPE school caused parents to bring/transfer their children to Cornerstone; most if not all were from neighbouring UPE schools'
• Good relationship among parents and teachers; parents easily monitor school activities and children's performance
• All pupils speak English as the official language, unlike in government schools
• Pupils are allowed to study on credit for some time to enable parents to find money
• 'Children are given breakfast and lunch, unlike in government schools. In government schools it has just been piloted, but might not work because of [the] large number of pupils.'
• Because of good teaching services and constant supervision of teachers by directors
• Because we do external examinations, especially exams from schools in Central Uganda
• Because rules and regulations in private schools are strictly followed; this makes parents feel that their children are safe
• Enrolment of cross-cultural pupils
• 'Because we have good rate of assessment compared to the neighbouring government school, this improves our performance in exams'
• 'Because we are not embracing the thematic curriculum and mother-tongue policy [teaching using local language in lower classes] like in government schools, hence parents are motivated to bring their children to this school because we teach in English.'
• Curriculum and syllabus are strictly followed
• 'We also expose pupils to mass media, tours to develop talents in all corners, which parents highly recommend and this is lacking in government schools.'
• 'Because this school has a conducive learning environment; no vehicle, noise etc.'

Parents on why they sent their children to private school

Why did you decide to send your children to private school?
• Standards and academic excellence; expectations being met fully – 'performance of my children has improved from what it was when they were in UPE school' • Children are made to speak English, even in P2 or lower classes • Competition is high; pupils are made to work harder by not being given exaggerated marks and not promoted to higher classes automatically • Teachers have a good relationship with pupils and encourage pupils who are not so active – unlike in government schools, where there is an 'I don't care' attitude • Strict supervision of teachers by the directors, which makes them perform better – no dodging lessons. • Children are promoted on merit, and the standard is high • Teachers are time conscious • The number of pupils is limited, which enables teachers to interact and know all pupils individually • Private schoolteachers have good discipline; a director would not want to have teachers who would spoil the image of the school • Pupils are taken for study tours, although at the parents' expense; parents of UPE schools do not understand and are never willing to do so, because they know everything [in the government school] is for free • Continuous assessments given to pupils, e.g. weekly, monthly, termly; children also also exposed to external exams (past papers are sourced from Kampala schools) • 'My children were doing poorly in [the] UPE school; that is why we sent them to private schools' • 'Private school pupils have discipline, because of closeness to teachers; they are forced to speak only in English, they respect their teachers because of them being role models'

Primary school pupils on choice of school

Interviewee:	AKICA, RACHAEL	Private school pupil
Details:	P6 pupil; Age: 12; Sex: Female	

What I like about my school:
School has very good teachers compared to neighbouring UPE schools
Schools environment is good for learning; has enough desks
Pupils are few, thus good discipline and we pay attention to the teacher in class

What I don't like about my school:
Some pupils do not want to speak English and are giving animal bones to carry, which is very bad
Sometimes we are not given enough food, or we miss food and even plates are not enough

Relationship with Canon Lawrence Demonstration Primary School (a government school):
I have some friends in that school, but I do not like anything or admire my friends in that school

Why parents sent her to Cornerstone (a private school):
Good performance of the school compared to the nearby schools

Interviewee:	RUMA, DANIEL	Private school pupil
Details:	P7 pupil; Age: 11; Sex: Male	

What I like about my school:
Good teaching
Teachers follow time and teach all subjects
Good sanitation – emphasis put on smartness
Pupils are provided food and water for drinking and hand washing
Clean toilet
Clean classrooms and not crowded
Clean environment; flowers make the school look so beautiful
Availability of textbooks, though some are missing
Pupils are disciplined and respectful to teachers
Enough playground

What I don't like about my school:
School is not fenced
Children do not have enough playground and balls are never available for both girls and boys
Water comes from the tap, which may give children disease

Relationship with Canon Lawrence Demonstration Primary School (a government school):
Has some friends in the government school
Football matches between the two schools

Why parents sent him to Cornerstone (a private school):
School is good
Population of pupils is limited
Children are very smart and disciplined
Teachers do not drink, [and] they do not miss lessons. They come to teach every day
School is near home

| Interviewee: | EMAN, RONALD | Government school pupil |
| Details: | P6 pupil; Age: 12; Sex: Male | |

What I like about my school:
Free education
Enough seats/desks for all pupils
Teachers are always punctual for lessons

What I don't like about my school:
No urinals, not enough toilets
No lunch provided for pupils
Children are over worked e.g. having to cut grass in the school grounds
What I like about the neighbouring private primary school:
Many toilets
The children have a nice smart uniform
They are served lunch at school

What I think children at private school like about my school:
Spacious playing ground
Pen-pal club is not in other schools
Participation in games and sports; Cornerstone seldom participates

Why I think my teachers are always punctual:
They are motivated by USh2,000 paid by each child per term

Why my parents sent me to government school:
Less costly in terms of school fees
Teachers are active and many

| Interviewee: | EJANG, HILDA | Government school pupil |
| Details: | P6 pupil; Age: 14; Sex: Female | |

What I like about my school:
Good singing club/school choir
Netball
General cleanliness and cleaning (dressing) room for older girls
Good performance
Gender sensitivity is observed i.e. only female teachers attend to girls regarding personal issues
Children's rights are observed

What I don't like about my school:
Boys are violent to girls – fighting
Some teachers use vulgar words, especially towards older girls, e.g. being insulted because of having big breasts; they say you are old enough to produce children
Most pupils are undisciplined – because of the large numbers, teachers cannot control all of them

Do you report these cases of teachers?
One case was reported, and parents during a PTA meeting cautioned the teacher

What I like about the neighbouring private primary school:
Dressing smartly
Better performance compared to us
Better feeding – porridge for breakfast and also served lunch

What I think children at private school like about my school:
Nice compound, covered with trees
Children's rights are observed; children are rarely beaten by teachers
Pupils are so many, which gives a good opportunity to create many friends

Why my parents sent me to government school:
Full-time electricity, even at night for revision
It is nearer home
It is affordable; we pay only 6,500 shillings per year

Interviewee:	JASPER	Government school pupil
Details:	P5 pupil; Age: 13; Sex: Male	

What I like about my school:
Effective teaching

What I don't like about my school:
Day pupils are being cheated in terms of learning time compared to pupils in [the] boarding section, who are even taught at night
What do you think can enhance your learning?
Availability of reading materials, especially simplified textbooks and pamphlets
Availability of sports attire, e.g. uniform, boots etc.

Why my parents sent me to government school:
School is nearer home
Children are friendly
Sports and games for all pupils

Interviewee:	ABWANGO, BENSON	Parent of pupil at government school
Details:	Sex: Male; Occupation: Peasant farmer	

'...I have two [children], both are boys; one is in P4 another in P2 ... they are both in Canon Lawrence [the UPE school]. I had to send them there, as you see my condition, you go for what is cheap...what your pocket can afford!'

'...because I wanted to enjoy free UPE provided by government; after all the government has used the taxes we pay in various ways to pay the teachers, so why do I have to pay teachers elsewhere again?.... I made the decision myself as head of the family to send both of them there...'

'Yes it is free education from government. I expect my children to study for free and that is good for a poor man like me.'

'It [UPE] is good, but corruption is spoiling its objectives... I hear that some money gets lost even before it reaches the school, and that some of the money is misused at school ... but generally, I am happy because I am not paying school fees and this is good for me...'

'I only pay development fund and PTA funds, which [are] less than 7,000 shillings per child per term...when the season is not bad, I can easily get that money... by selling a basin of groundnuts per term... and of course buying for them pencils and books.... since they spoil the books and loose pencils almost every week, I have to buy others!'

'... I think government schools have many teachers, large classrooms and generally we pay less money [compared to the private schools] ...and the members of the school management are selected from us – the parents ...although this is mainly the rich parents who are selected.'

'... Well, there are a few things, for example I don't like the way they sometimes transfer good teachers, ... even without consulting us, you just hear that teacher so-and-so has now been transferred to another school! I do not know whether that is a punishment from the Ministry (of Education and Sports) or a grudge with the district people, so they send that teacher to a bad school... Also the school is not well renovated, for example the walls are very dirty, it seems classrooms are not cleaned ... my children come back every day with very dirty uniforms, yet they have chairs!... and the latrines are very dirty... Teachers are always complaining of late salary payments, which affects their work of teaching ...'

Interviewee:	Ms. ASIIMWE, JENNIFER	Parent of pupil at private school
Details:	Sex: Female; Occupation: Secretary – single parent	
	Number of children: 3; Children in private school: 1 (P4, a girl)	

Why did you choose to send your child to a private school?
Good and constant teaching
School near home – reduces distance
School is morally good; no harassment of children, no theft, pupils are protected compared to government schools
Conducive environment for learning

Understanding of UPE:
Everything about it is negative; children are not under control and not well guided
Classes are overcrowded
Poor teaching; slow learners are not considered, which makes parents opt for private schools
Harassment by other pupils, because of large number of pupils
No protection by teachers
Teachers don't give assignments or mark pupils' books

Only good thing about UPE:
Free education, but very expensive in the long run. Experience she had from her daughter studying in a UPE school: 'she couldn't write, read or speak a single word in English, yet she was in P5! I moved her to a private school and she was demoted to P4'

What I like about private schools:
Teachers committed to teaching
Results-oriented and sometimes they teach over to finish the syllabus
Teachers [are] very hardworking in fear of dismissal
They have strategic locations, which provide [a] good learning environment with no noise
Good [food] given to children, which makes them feel at home
Classes are not so crowded; limited number of children
Good structures and regular renovation
Keen on welfare and health of children
Easy access, as it is nearer home
Good moral upbringing of children in the school; children taught how to pray

What I dislike about private schools:
Sometimes children harassed if fees not cleared early enough, which may make a child miss exams
Everything is about money, thus sometimes management doesn't listen to pleas of parents
Sometimes management and directors are aggressive to teachers – they don't listen, which makes teachers' work under a lot of tension
Short-term contracts given to teachers could demoralise [them]

Gaps in Cornerstone (my daughter's private school):
Wrangle over money by the proprietors
Accountability not given to parents
Delay in paying staff salaries
Sometimes school closes early, because director doesn't want to release money to buy food, clean water bills
Some parents don't bring or take [a] long [time] to bring food items for school feeding

Proprietor of Cornerstone (private) Primary School

Background to the school's establishment:
- Four neighbouring secondary schoolteachers joined together and started the school as a nursery school for their children in 2000
- School started as a nursery school, with seven children (four belonging to the proprietors), but had 20 pupils by end of the first term
- School started with two teachers, who were well motivated
- Parents of children requested that the proprietor open a primary section because of good performance, discipline and smartness of pupils
- Primary section was opened in 2002
- PTA was formed in 2001; it helped in starting the primary section. PTA helped in mobilising the community, who came to support the school, including the Church of Uganda
- Got a loan of 2 million shillings from Stanbic Land. Land cost USh400,000; 1.6 million shillings used to start up construction work, plus personal contributions by proprietors

Motivation for starting school:
- Children were hungry in school; this affected their performance in class. They did a mini survey before opening a primary section
- Availability of spacious land
- Poor performance of UPE schools
- Demand by parents for a school within the community, so as to avoid children travelling the distance into town
- Wanted another source of making money
- Requests made by parents of children in nursery section
- Population of 'working class' parents is high; they prefer their children to stay for a long time in school
- Scholarships are given to best performers in each class, who then study for free the following terms; others given gifts, e.g. books etc.
- Keenness on children looking smart

School management:
- Board of Directors (BOD), which is the supreme administrative organ – four teachers
- The Parent Teacher Association (PTA)
- Recruitment of teachers is done by BOD; here emphasis is placed on teachers having a minimum grade 3 certificate
- Head teachers, for primary and nursery sections, are in charge of running daily activities/implementation, supported by deputy head teachers, directors of studies and by teachers
- Each of the four directors are assigned different roles and responsibilities:
    Director in charge of finance: supervises the bursar, follows up head teacher on payment of fees etc.
    Director in charge of welfare, i.e. both for pupils and teachers
    Director of infrastructural development, e.g. construction work
    BOD Chairman supervises all directors and co-ordinators all activities, he is the official spokesperson of the school
- Some children are being funded under the Church of Uganda by Compassion International in both nursery and primary for five years
- No financial and material support from government

Current standing:
- Grade of school: 4
- Teacher-pupil ratio 1:56
- Nine teachers (three female and six male)
- Nursery school and primary schoolteachers are being trained at the school's expense – 17 student teachers: 12 women and five men are currently being trained
- No examination centre yet, mainly due to lack of examination hall
- School not yet graded, but registered: grading is done by MoES in consultation with UNEB, who do the registration
- The school status is mixed primary school with nine qualified teachers and seven classrooms

School is registered under the following conditions:
- Trained registered teachers
- Training materials, e.g. classroom, books etc.
- Adequate space
- Minimum of 15 children

Future plans:
- Intend to make the school boarding only
- Construct more infrastructure
- Introduce computer learning and study into the curriculum
- Life skills, e.g. agriculture
- Provide quality education cheaply, using available local resources
- Having an orderly compound that provides a learning environment

Relationship with neighbouring UPE schools:
- Enjoys good working relationship
- From 2005–06, candidates of Cornerstone did their exams at Canon Lawrence Demonstration School
- Have held friendly debates, which sustain the relationship
- Even the children of teachers, including the headmistress of Canon Lawrence Demonstration School, study at Cornerstone
- Some teachers from neighbouring UPE schools help foster teaching at Cornerstone during weekends
- Some teachers from government schools do visit, as part of a programme called 'team teaching.' This is a method where teachers jointly prepare lessons, i.e. one presents and the rest monitor/listen, and then later discuss and make necessary changes. This has assisted those teachers who are not well versed with some topics
- Cornerstone is performing better than neighbouring government schools in primary leaving examination (PLE) and is appreciated by community
- Quality of education in Cornerstone is far better, e.g. availability of books, English-speaking and debates

Relationship with District Education Department:
- Inspection by District Inspector of Schools; occasionally the Centre Co-ordination Tutor (CCT) visits the school; on a few occasions, one or two teachers are invited to attend district-level workshops, especially on the curriculum
- Visits by District Education Officer (DEO) staff are mostly for inspection of school activities; this typically includes giving conditions on the number of teachers, desks, construction of latrines etc. Such visits are rarely for professional development

- The school follows the same syllabus as government schools. In addition, the government examination timetable and school calendar are also followed. However, the school does more than the government-stipulated extra curricula activities, such as debating clubs and environment clubs
- The thematic policy and method of teaching lower classes (P1–P3) in local language is only used once in a while; it is not effective and not much welcomed

Challenges:
- Insufficient funds to construct adequate infrastructure
- School not yet to full standard, because classes have rough floors and window shutters
- Paying teachers' salaries
- Meeting community expectations and aspirations of producing better results – so the school even teaches on weekends; P6 and P7 pupils are now staying in the boarding section
- Reading materials – books and instruction materials hard to acquire
- Ability to absorb growing enrolment, while maintaining a manageable teacher-pupil ratio. The mission of the school is to have a classroom manageable by a teacher (1:45). If the number is bigger, classes are divided into streams
- Retention of teachers – they leave any time if they get a better offer

Interviewee:	MZEE, JOHN ATIA OTIM	Retired Education Civil Servant
Details:	76 years old	

The state of private schools in Uganda:
- Quality of education varies across the three categories of private, community and public schools
- Private schools tend to focus more on high scores than real learning
- What is the value of a private school amidst UPE schools?
- The value of a private school is that the UPE school can't satisfy everybody – government schools only serve the interests of the poor people
- They give satisfaction to people who can afford to pay for their children's education

Advantages of private schools over UPE schools:
- If well supervised, private schools provide high-quality education and results, especially if initiated and owned by people with an educational vision and life objectives
- They put a lot of emphasis on the creation of conducive learning conditions

Weaknesses of private schools:
- Most of them put a lot on emphasis on monetary gain – they have a profit-driven attitude, which in most cases compromises their primary objectives
- They tend to focus more on results, so as to attract more children to their school, whereas education should be holistic. They seldom consider children's personal development and growth

Weaknesses of government schools:
- Weak government policy, e.g. the introduction of PLE was faulty in terms of policy, planning, timing and structure. No consideration was given to teacher-pupil ratios, number of textbooks, number of classrooms etc.
- The schools are getting overwhelmed by the number of children per class
- Children are not being considered properly; they cannot read, write and speak even in their local language

Positive side of government schools:
- Having large number of children provides a good opportunity for social interaction and togetherness
- Free education to poor children
- Most teachers are professionally well trained

Areas of improvement in government schools:
- Increasing number of classrooms, number of teachers, desks, textbooks etc.
- Improvement in PLE system should begin from above, i.e. from ministerial/policy level down to school administration level
- Primary teachers' colleges should admit only those students who pass 'O' level (senior 4) well and should initiate a system of follow-up, supervision and monitoring of teachers who pass through their colleges. There are so many cases of people who join these colleges with 'borrowed' academic papers from friends or relatives. Such 'fools' later become 'teachers' and end up fostering the next generation of 'fools' in the classes that they teach. It is not a surprise that we have many children failing their primary school exams

Improvement – private schools:
- They should recruit teachers of substance, not 'rejects'
- They should start having a career master/mistress to guide children, other than just putting emphasis on academic excellence and high results
- The aim of private education should be filling gaps left by government schools. They should therefore include parents in school administration; parents and the general community should be involved in the activities of such schools to ensure dual ownership

Role of parents and community:
- Parents and the general community should collectively know that school ownership is their role. They should thus show interest by participating in school activities, since it is for the benefit of their children
- Parents and community alike should help train children and behave responsibly towards them at all times

Historically in Lango sub-region:
Private education started in the 1960s. Private schools played a crucial role in the development of education in Lango sub-region. By the early 1960s, there were two private primary schools: Canon Dongo P.S in Boroboro and Okae Jepenia P.S. in Aduku. Such schools absorbed children of the elite and those who could not travel to distant schools; government schools were very few at that time. For example, Hon Charles Odyek Okot (RIP) the first MP from Lango West in Uganda's first parliament, excelled through private primary school up to university.

Conclusions

There is an important role for private schools in achieving EFA alongside public education (UPE). The government alone may not be able to cope with the demand for basic education and therefore needs non-state actors such as private individuals, institutions and non-governmental organisations to contribute to achieving EFA. Public education alone may not be adequate to guarantee all children access to quality education, because of resource constraints in the public sector. It is these gaps in public education that the private schools fill. Private schools can help to achieve EFA through proper regulation, supervision and government support in both financial and material terms.

Conversion of community schools into government schools

In response to the sudden and dramatic expansion in pupil's enrolment, the Ugandan government embarked on owning more schools, mainly by taking over formerly community-founded schools. The figure below shows that following the massive enrolment in the 1996-97, the Government of Uganda responded by establishing close to 2,000 primary schools between 1997 and 1999 alone.

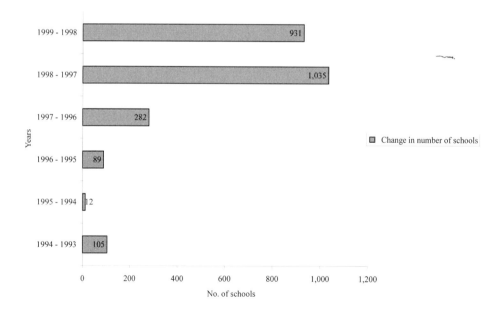

Figure 6.2 Change in the number of schools in Uganda 1993–1999
Source: UNESCO (2000) The EFA Assessment 2000 Country Report: Uganda

Management of private schools in Uganda

Every school owner is mandated to manage his/her school in a manner in which the objectives of education are supreme. The owner charges school dues as prescribed by the Management Committee/Board of Governors. Designated government officials may issue instructions on aspects of school management, with a view to safeguarding the interests of pupils. Every school is required to prepare an annual budget estimate and annual audited accounts. On request by designated officials, these documents should be availed for inspection. This means private schools in Uganda are not autonomous or independent, despite being non-state entities. Private schools are bound by rules set by the Ministry of Education.

Procedures for establishing private schools

Procedures for establishing a private school include application to the permanent secretary or chief administration officer/town clerk on evidence of good repute and necessary funds to manage the institution. Entrepreneurs then seek permission from local authorities at sub-county level. This is to find out whether it is within the Sub-County Development Plan to have a school where the entrepreneur plans to establish one, to ensure that the school's plans are reflected in the overall Education Development Plan of the respective area, and that the school plans meet the educational needs of the country or the area. The sub-county officials then recommend the entrepreneur to the district authorities. The District Inspector inspects the site for the new school to check whether it fulfils regulations. Other requirements for registration include the following:

Possession of building plans, lease offers and/or land titles;

- Adequate school facilities, including physical structures like classrooms, latrines, school furniture and enough land for a playground;

- Classrooms and latrines;

- A 'suitably qualified' head teacher, and evidence that the teachers to be engaged are eligible to teach in the type of school (teachers trained to grade 2 and 3 certificate level);

- Adequate terms and conditions of service of employment for teaching and non-teaching staff, with contractual terms of agreement;

- The school will not refuse admission to any pupil on any discriminatory grounds;

- Short- and long-term school plans;

- A management and governance body constituted in accordance with government guidelines;

- Financial strength/financial statement; and

- Other bodies e.g. Parent Teacher Association, school management committee to create checks and balance etc.

Language policy

The use of mother tongue as the language for instruction comes with a couple of challenges: some districts do not have written orthography, while others do not even have district language boards. The dearth of instructional and learning materials in the local language poses yet another challenge. In urban and peri-urban areas (and in districts which have many tribal settlements), choice of 'the mother tongue' is not obvious; similarly, the posting and distribution of trained teachers does not favour equitable distribution of personnel across the country. So far in Uganda, there has been very limited training of teachers in the use of mother-tongue/local language as a medium of instruction.

Notes

1. Ministry of Education and Sports (MoES, 2003a).
2. Ibid.
3. £1 was equivalent to USh3373.26 in January 2008.
4. Interview with proprietor of private school in Mbale town.
5. MoES (2003a).
6. Ibid.
7. Interviews with District Inspector of Schools, Lira District.
8. Ministry of Education and Sports (2003b).
9. MoES (2003a).
10. Ministry of Education and Sports: Sector PEAP Revision Paper (November 2003).
11. Ibid.
12. Ministry of Education and Sport (2002a).
13. Ministry of Education and Sport (2002b).
14. It was erroneously assumed that by 2007 all community schools would be 'converted' into government schools.
15. This is estimated to be about 68 per cent of overall national expenditure on education. The Indicative Medium Term Expenditure Framework FY 2003/04–2006/07 places total expenditure on the education sub-sector (including donor and projects) at USh723.87 billion in financial year (FY) 2006/07, with primary education teachers wages projected at USh258.12 billion (Oct 2003) and primary education conditional grants and district development grants estimated at USh47.90 billion and USh65.2 billion respectively.
16. MoES (2002a).
17. In the Ugandan system, a grade 3 teacher's certificate is the minimum requirement to teach in lower primary school. All teachers must also hold a Uganda certificate of education with credits in at least two science subjects, English and maths. This is the result of four years of

secondary education. The grade 3 teacher's course takes two years and is conducted in primary teachers' colleges (previously known as teachers' training colleges). The grade 4 teacher's certificate is a one-year course for upper primary schools. This can then be followed on with a three-year upgrading course, which leads to the grade 5 certificate for secondary school teachers.

18. EMIS Annual Census, 2006.

19. Interview with District Inspector of Schools, Lira district, 2007.

20. Ministry of Education and Sport *Education Abstracts 2004.*

21. Ministry of Education and Sport *Education abstracts 2006.*

22. Kitaev, I. (1999).

23. The annual primary school calendar in Uganda consists of three terms of 10–13 weeks each.

24. Currently Uganda has 70 districts, with Northern Uganda constituting 41 per cent of the total number of districts.

25. With respect to Uganda, 'class' is used to denote children's year group whereas 'grade' is used with respect to teacher's qualification and 'grade' of school.

26. Ministry of Education and Sport (2006).

27. MoES (2002b).

28. EMIS *Annual Census 2007.* This table was developed from data for 178 (out of 214) government and two (out of nine) private primary schools.

29. EMIS (2006).

30. This figure includes 11 schools whose ownership status was not stated.

31. Ibid.

32. Ibid.

33. MoES (2002a).

34. Interview with District Inspector of Schools, Lira.

35. Excerpts of an interview held with the District Inspector of Schools, Lira District, and the director of a private school.

36. *Uganda DHS EdData Survey 2001.*

37. Data that was accessed during the study did not have adequate information on the quality of infrastructure.

38. Grade I is the highest grade and denotes a school with most of the required facilities and personnel in place.

39. As recommended by Government Education Policy, P4 is average nine years of age while P7 is average 12 years of age.

40. Government policy states that the language of instruction for P1–P4 should be mother tongue.

References

Adediran, S (2007) *Private Sector Education in Nigeria*. A brief for DFID's ESSPIN (Education Sector Support Programme in Nigeria) Education Group. London, UK: Department for International Development.

Adelabu, M and P Rose (2004) 'Non-State Provision of Basic Education in Nigeria' in G Larbi et al (ed.) *Nigeria: Study of Non-State Providers of Basic Services*. University of Birmingham, UK: International Development Department.

Aggarwal, Y (2000) *Public and private partnership in primary education in India: A study of unrecognised schools in Haryana*. New Delhi, India: National Institute of Educational Planning and Administration.

Belfield, C and HM Levin (2002) *Educational Privatization: Causes, Consequences and Planning Implications*. Paris, France: United Nations Educational, Scientific and Cultural Organization (UNESCO). Available at: http://www.unesco.org/iiep/PDF/Fund74.pdf [accessed 6 May 2008]

Bray, M (1999) *Adverse effects of private supplementary tutoring: dimensions, implications and government responses*. Paris, France: UNESCO.

Catholic Relief Services (CRS) (2006) 'Educational Quality Improvement Programme (EQUIP): Phased and cluster based approach to education quality improvement.' A programme designed by Subir Shukla and implemented by CRS: process documentation and assessment. Lucknow, India.

Center for Applied Linguistics (CAL) (2004) *Expanding Education Opportunity in Linguistically Diverse Society*. Washington DC, USA: CAL. Available at: http://www.cal.org/resources/pubs/expandexec.html [accessed 22 April 2008]

Centre for Civil Society (2007) *Education for the Poor: Survey Report*. New Delhi, India: Centre for Civil Society. Available at: http://www.ccsindia.org/pdf/surveyreport.pdf [accessed 22 April 2008]

Chediel, RW, N Sekwao and PL Kirumba (2000) *Private and community schools in Tanzania (Mainland)*. Paris, France: UNESCO.

Chittibabu, SV (2003) SV Chittibabu Commission report. Tamil Nadu: Government of Tamil Nadu.

De, Anuradha et al (1999) Public Report on Basic Education (PROBE). New Delhi, India: Oxford University Press.

De, A, C Noronha and M Samson (2002a) 'Private Schools for Less Privileged: Some Insights from a Case Study' in *Economic and Political Weekly*, 37 (52), pp.5230-5236.

De, A, M Majumdar, M Samson and C Noronha (2002b) 'Role of Private Schools in Basic Education,' in R Govinda (ed.) *India Education Report*. New Delhi, India: Oxford University Press.

De Stefano, J (2006) Meeting EFA: Zambia Community Schools. Washington DC, USA: EQUIP2. Available at: http://www.equip123.net/docs/e2-ZambiaCaseStudy.pdf [accessed 22 April 2008]

District Information System for Education (DISE) (2006). Available at: http://www.dpepmis.org/ [accessed 22 April 2008]

Federal Ministry of Education (2004a) Nigeria Education Sector Analysis – Monitoring of Learning Achievement Project 2003: Assessment of Learning Achievement of Primary Four and Primary Six Pupils. Abuja, Nigeria: Federal Ministry of Education.

Federal Ministry of Education (2004b) National Policy on Education (revised). Abuja, Nigeria: Federal Ministry of Education.

Federal Ministry of Education (2006) *Basic and Senior Secondary Education Statistics in Nigeria, 2004 and 2005.* Abuja, Nigeria: Federal Ministry of Education.

Josephine, Y (1999) *School efficiency and policy of resource planning: a pilot study on Mysore high schools.* New Delhi, India: NIEPA (National Institute of Educational Planning and Administration).

Kingdon, Geeta (1996a) 'The quality and efficiency of private and public education: A case study of urban India,' in *Oxford Bulletin of Economics and Statistics* 58.1: pp.57–81.

Kingdon, Geeta (1996b) *Private schooling in India: Size, nature and equity-effects.* London, UK: London School of Economics, Development Economics Programme.

Kingdon, Geeta (2005) Private and public schooling: The Indian experience. Draft paper. Available at: http://www.ksg.harvard.edu/pepg/PDF/events/MPSPE/PEPG-05-15geeta.pdf%20w [accessed 22 April 2008]

Kitaev, I (1999) *Private Education in Sub-Saharan Africa: A re-examination of theories and concepts related to its development and finance.* Paris, France: UNESCO.

Komarek, K (2003) *Universal Primary Education in Multilingual Societies.* Eschborn, Germany: Association for Development of Education in Africa (ADEA) and GTZ. Available at: http://www2.gtz.de/dokumente/bib/04-5238.pdf [accessed 22 April 2008]

Kremer, M, K Muralidharan, N Chaudhury, J Hammer and FH Rogers (2004) *Teacher Absence in India.* Washington DC, USA: World Bank. Available at: http://siteresources.worldbank.org/DEC/Resources/36660_Teacher_absence_in_India_EEA_9_15_04_-_South_Asia_session_version.pdf [accessed 6 May 2008]

Majumdar, M (2003) 'Financing of Basic Education: Private Solution to Public Deficiency?' in JBG Tilak (ed.) *Financing Education in India: Current Issues and Changing Perspectives.* New Delhi, India: NIEPA and Ravi Books.

Mandava, N (2007) *The Unknown Education Revolution in India.* Mint, The Hindustan Times, 8 March 2007, p.23. Available at: http://indianeconomy.org/2007/03/09/the-unknown-education-revolution-in-india/[accessed 22 April 2008]

McIntosh, N (2005) 'Breaking the State Monopoly in the Provision of Schooling'. Conference on Mobilising the Private Sector for Public Education. Washington DC, USA: World Bank. Available at: http://www.ksg.harvard.edu/pepg/PDF/events/MPSPE/MPSPE_Agenda.pdf [accessed 22 April 2008]

Mehrotra, S and R Parthasarthi (2006) 'Private Provision of Elementary Education in India: Findings of a Survey in Eight States,' in *Compare: A Journal of Comparative Education*, 36, 4, pp.421–442.

Mehta, A (2005) Elementary education in unrecognised schools in India: a study of Punjab based on DISE 2005 data. New Delhi, India: National Institute of Educational Planning and Administration.

Mehta, A (2007) Elementary education in India: progress towards UEE. DISE Analytical Report, 2005-2006. New Delhi, India: National University of Educational Planning and Administration.

Ministry of Education and Sports (MoES) (2001) *Education Sector Fact-file 2001*. Kampala, Uganda: MoES.

Ministry of Education and Sport (2002a) Country Proposal for Education for All By 2015 Fast Track Initiative. Kampala, Uganda: MoES.

Ministry of Education and Sport (2002b) Progress Report on Education Management Information System (EMIS). Kampala, Uganda: MoES.

Ministry of Education and Sport (2003a) Poverty Eradication Action Plan, Revision Paper November 2003. Kampala, Uganda: MoES.

Ministry of Education and Sport (2003b) Ninth Education Sector Review: Aide Memoire. Kampala, Uganda: MoES.

Ministry of Education and Sport (MoES) (2004) *Education in Uganda: Uganda Educational Statistics Abstract Volume 1*. Kampala, Uganda: MoES

Ministry of Education and Sport (MoES) (2006) *Education in Uganda: Uganda Educational Statistics Abstract Volume 1*. Kampala, Uganda: MoES.

Muralidharan, K and M Kremer (2006) Public and Private Schools in Rural India. Boston, USA: Harvard University. Available at: http://www.people.fas.harvard.edu/~muralidh/Public_and_Private_Schools_in_Rural_India_032206.pdf [accessed 6 May 2008]

Nicolai S (2005) Fragment Foundation: Education and Chronic Crisis in the Occupied Palestinian Territory. Paris, France: UNESCO. Available at: http://unesdoc.unesco.org/images/0015/001502/150260e.pdf [accessed 22 April 2008]

Parliamentary Research Service (2005) The Right to Education Bill, 2005.

Pratham (2006) *Annual Status of Education Report (ASER) 2005*. India: Pratham.

Pratichi Trust (2002) *The Delivery of Primary Education: A Study in West Bengal*. New Delhi, India: The Pratichi Trust Team, Pratichi (India) Trust.

Press Trust of India (2007) 'Private schools can't bridge education gap'. News item, 20 December 2007.

Shukla, S. (2007) *Advancement of Educational Performance Through Teacher Support, (ADEPTS)*. New Delhi, India: Ministry of Human Resource Development and UNICEF.

Smith, I and S Musoke (2006) 'A Study On Deployment, Utilisation and Management Of Secondary Education Teachers Under UPPET.' Kampala, Uganda: Ministry of Education and Sport.

Srivastava, P (2007) Neither Voice nor Loyalty: School Choice and the Low-Fee Private Sector in India. Research Publications Series, Occasional Paper No.134. New York, USA: National Centre for the Study of Privatization in Education, Columbia University.

Tilak, JBG (2004) 'Public Subsidies in the Education Sector in India' in *Economic and Political Weekly*, 39 (4) (24-30 January 2004): pp.343-59.

Tooley, J (2000) The Private Sector Serving the Educational Needs of the Poor. Paper delivered at Asian Development Bank Institute Conference, 2000. Available at: http://www.ncl.ac.uk/egwest/people/james.tooley/Tokyo%20seminar%20.doc [accessed 23 April 2008]

Tooley, J (2001) 'Serving the needs of the poor: The private education sector in developing countries' in C. Hepburn (ed.) *Can the market save our schools* (pp.167–184). Vancouver, Canada: Fraiser Institute.

Tooley J (2005a) *Is private education good for the poor?* Newcastle, UK: University of Newcastle.

Tooley, J (2005b) Private Schools Serving the Poor, Working Paper: A Study from Delhi, India. New Delhi, India: Centre for Civil Society.

Tooley, J (2006) Educating Amaretch: Private Schools for the Poor and the New Frontier for investment. International Finance Corporation (IFC) and *Financial Times* Gold Prize Essay, 2006. Available at: http://www.ifc.org/ifcext/economics.nsf/AttachmentsByTitle/educating_amaretch_booklet.pdf/$FILE/educating_amaretch_booklet.pdf [accessed 23 April 2008]

Tooley, J and P Dixon (2003) *Private schools for the poor: A case study from India.* Reading, UK: CfBT Research and Development.

Tooley, J and P Dixon (2006) "De facto' privatisation of education and the poor: implications of a study from sub-Saharan Africa and India' in *Compare* Vol.36, No.4, December 2006, pp.443–462. Available at: http://www.ncl.ac.uk/egwest/pdfs/Compare.pdf [accessed 23 April 2008]

Uganda Bureau of Statistics (UBS) (2001) DHS EdData Survey, 2001 Education Data for Decision-making. Entebbe, Uganda: UBS. Available at: http://www.dhseddata.com/rpt/UgandaEdData.PDF [accessed 6 May 2008]

UNESCO (2000) Education For All: The Year 2000 Assessment Report of Uganda. Available at: http://www.unesco.org/education/wef/countryreports/uganda/contents.html#cont

United Nations Office for the Coordination of Humanitarian Affairs, Integrated Regional Information Networks (IRIN). See: http://www.irinnews.org/ [accessed 23 April 2008].

UN Population Division (2006) World Population Prospects: The 2006 Revision Population Database. Available at: http://esa.un.org/unpp/ [accessed 6 May 2008]

World Bank Independent Evaluation Group (2006) *From schooling access to learning outcomes: An unfinished agenda.* An evaluation of World Bank support to primary education. Washington DC, USA: World Bank.

World Bank (2003) World Development Report 2004: 'Making Services Work for Poor People.' Washington DC, USA: World Bank.

World Bank Kennedy School of Government & Harvard University (2005) *Mobilizing the Private Sector for Public Education.* Washington DC, USA.

Index

learning aids 114
levies 69, 111–12
Levin, HM 21–2
LGA (local government authority) secretaries 121–3
literacy 67, 68, 102
local government authority (LGA) secretaries 121–3
low-cost, meaning 1, 7–10, 41

Majumdar, M 55, 78
management
    government schools 19, 45–6
    private schools 163, 169
Mandava, N 46
market conditions 16
MDGs *see* Millennium Development Goals
Medium-Term Budget Framework (MTBF) 133, 150
Mehrotra, S 78
Mehta, A 38, 50–3, 57, 72, 74–5, 81, 87
methodology 2, 10–13
    Nigerian study 95–6
    Ugandan study 138–9
Millennium Development Goals (MDGs)
    Nigeria 92, 93
    Uganda 131, 132
Ministry of Education and Sports (MoES) data 139–45
Monitoring of Learning Achievement 97, 100–2
mother tongue 170
    see also language of instruction
motivation for school ownership 34, 63, 74, 163
MTBF (Medium-Term Budget Framework) 133, 150
Muralidharan, K 49, 56, 76–7, 87–8

National Capital Region of Delhi 64–9
National University of Educational Planning and Administration (NUEPA) 43
NEMIS (Nigerian Education Management Information System) 91
net enrolment ratio (NER) 15–16, 132
Nigeria 3–4, 91–129
    case studies 104–27

focus groups 112–14, 116–25
    summary 125–7
data analysis 97–102
Education Management Information System 10
enrolment rates 3, 15–16, 93, 97–100, 105, 107–8
focus groups 112–25
    local government authority secretaries 121–3
    owners 121
    parents 116–20
    pupils 123–5
    teachers 112–14
    teachers' union 123
literature 92–5
primary school statistics 97–102
private sector summary 102–4
school categorisation 91
study methodology 95–6
Nigeria Union of Teachers (NUT) 123
Nigerian Education Management Information System (NEMIS) 91
non-government schools 7–8, 10–11, 38–9
Noronha, C 78
NUEPA (National University of Educational Planning and Administration) 43
numeracy tests 100–1
NUT (Nigeria Union of Teachers) 123

Ogun case study 104–27
opening periods 59, 64
opinion leader interview 166–7
out-of-school children 15, 52–3, 133
owners 1
    case studies 121, 163–5
    motivation 34, 63, 74, 163
    qualifications 59, 60

Parent Teacher Associations (PTAs) 112
parents
    challenges 153
    choice 22–4, 26
        India 56–7, 76
        Nigeria 116
        Uganda 145–8, 156–7
    education 56, 67, 68
    focus groups 116–20